The Noon Book of Authentic
Indian Cooking

The Noon Book of Authentic
Indian Cooking

G.K. Noon

Foreword by
Delia Smith

TUTTLE PUBLISHING
Boston · Rutland, Vermont · Tokyo

Foreword

I have known Noon (no one knows him as anything else) for ten years and it's thanks to him that I once—for the only time in my life—cheated on my dinner guests. Hidden in the kitchen were a variety of packs of his wonderful, factory-made curries. I didn't actually claim dinner was homemade, but my guests assumed it was and at the end I got embarrassing and very genuine compliments on the flavor and authenticity of the meal. It was all done in the cause of research for an article and when you see the quality, care, and inventiveness that go into Noon's production process, you can understand why such praise is entirely deserved.

To have created authenticity in his ready-meal range—spices are bought whole by the ton and roasted precisely and to order—is Noon's abiding achievement. This book takes us even further, on a firsthand journey through the regions and cultures of India, to bring in the dazzling flavors of the subcontinent in classic dishes and in lesser known local specialities. All of them make you want to go straight to the kitchen and start grinding a few spices, and all of them carry Noon's trademark—authenticity.

Delia Smith

Introduction G.K. Noon

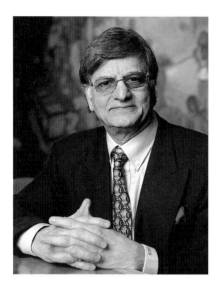

I have spent my entire working life in the food business—and it has left me hungry for more! My mother was an excellent cook and I can still remember the aroma of her Indian and Persian cooking—her family came from Shiraz in Iran. I especially remember the shrimp that she bought fresh which she then peeled; she was a discerning woman who placed great emphasis on good food and good company.

I am passionate about food and enjoy nothing better than to cook for a group of friends. I am delighted to share my enthusiasm for Indian food with you through the recipes in this book. They are authentic recipes that my mother would have recognized were she still alive. Each recipe has been perfected by the chefs at Noon Products, and it is recipes such as these that have helped fuel the growth of our company. They are tried and tested and easy to use.

Indian food is immensely popular in this country. With the demands of increasingly well-traveled and sophisticated consumers in mind, the master chefs at Noon can spend up to six months developing a single recipe. Each recipe reflects its provenance in the authentic ingredients and cooking methods used.

This book offers a wide cross-section of Indian food, from the Moghlai cuisine of North India and the vegetarian delights of Madras, to the fish specialities of the Malabar Coast, and many others. I hope you will enjoy the adventure of cooking them in your own kitchen. It's a slice of India that I am sure you will relish. Enjoy cooking.

The Noon chefs, from left to right:

B. Sainath Rao
Puneet Arora
Rakesh Yadav
Mr Ashok Kaul
Vishal Rew
Sumit Malik

Contents

KASHMIR

DELHI ●

BENGAL
● CALCUTTA

Bay of Bengal

MUMBAI ●
(Bombay)

● HYDERABAD

GOA

Arabian
Sea

● CHENNAI
(Madras)

Regions of India

by Mohini Kent

If what we eat describes who we are, then India is a baffling place, its menus dictated by the vagaries of history, caste, community, religion, and region.

Indian history is a long litany of strange names—Dravidian, Aryan, Buddhist, Greek, Muslim, Parsee, Sikh, Portuguese, French, Dutch, and English names—a story of migration, of blood and greed, of conquest and intrigue, of evangelical missionaries and moral crusaders. Even men of God who built empires of the spirit have helped to shape the cuisine. The country is the world's biggest food bazaar.

The Indian landscape, too, is a study in contrasts. From the highest mountain in the world, the Everest, to the dry, arid desert of Rajasthan, lush jungles and long, tropical coastlines, the local availability of green vegetables, grains, meat and fish have helped to mold eating habits as much as religious taboo. There are those who eat only wheat and others who eat only rice; some cook in *ghee* (clarified butter) but others use only coconut oil. Northerners drink tea from Assam but in the south they drink coffee from the great estates of Coorg and Ooty.

Legend has it that the first immigrants to India, the Dravidians, arrived about 9000 B.C. from a land that sank into the sea. Then, between the 4th and 2nd millennium B.C., came the Aryans, a semi-nomadic, pastoral people who lived chiefly on the produce of the sacred cow and for whom eating beef was taboo.

South India

The lighter-skinned Aryans pushed the dark-skinned Dravidians south of the Vindhya mountain range that neatly divides India into two. In the south, Tamil cities such as Chennai (formerly Madras) on the eastern Coromandel Coast preserved Dravidian culture and great temples grew into centers of the arts such as sculpture and the classical Bharata Natyam dance. Rice and dal (lentils) remain at the heart of their cuisine—although it is by no means all vegetarian. The climate is hot—and then it gets hotter!—and food is spicy.

On the western Malabar coast, St. Thomas the Apostle is believed to have arrived some years after the death of Jesus and converted India's first Christians. Centuries later, the Portuguese brought their own, more brutal Catholicism to the coast, followed by the Dutch, Loreto, and Carmelite nuns, and large communities of Christians still live there. It was the dream of William Wilberforce, the

were traders and shipbuilders who built ships for the English during the Napoleonic wars. The Parsees have no inhibitions about diet, although they abstain from eating beef out of respect for Hindus, and their cooking represents a fusion of Persian and Indian, their most famous dish being *dhansak* (meat with lentils). The pomegranate, symbol of fertility, and the date, symbolic of the tree of life, are included in Parsee feasts in memory of their days in Iran, but the rice, fish and coconut in their food are distinctly Indian additions.

The Portuguese Vasco de Gama arrived in Calicut on the Malabar Coast in 1498 A.D. looking for "christians and spices." A decade later the Portuguese had captured Goa and there they stayed until 1961. In religion, the Portuguese were intolerant and mass conversions by Franciscan and Jesuit missionaries have left Goa half-Catholic. Portuguese married local women after converting them, a strategy intended to produce a large Portuguese-Catholic population. All things Portuguese were highly prized, including olives and olive oil. Now Goa is a good mix of Hindu, Muslim, and Portuguese culture. Different ingredients and different cooking methods distinguish the cuisine of one community from another. For example, Goans of Portuguese Catholic descent will use vinegar and eat roast suckling pig while Goan Hindus prefer to use tamarind or lime juice as souring agents and prefer to eat chicken or mutton. Both communities relish the plentiful fish.

Kerala, in the very south of India, is also home to the traditional system of Ayurveda that uses herbal medicine to cure illness. It is a holistic approach, recognizing the role of the mind in healing the body and the dynamic play of the three elements of fire, water, and air in the individual. Ayurveda doctors use herbs and spices to bring about that balance in the body necessary for optimum health.

antislavery campaigner, to convert the whole of India to Christianity, but Christians remain about three percent of the population. Their cuisine has developed according to local taste but, since they have few or no taboos, it is quite distinct. For example, *appam*, the rice pancake of Kerala, would be eaten with *aviyal* (vegetables in coconut milk) by the Hindu Nair community, but the Syrian Christians could eat it with beef stew.

The earliest Jews came to India in ancient times but the Cochin Jews arrived in the 1st century A.D., fleeing persecution by the Romans. Their numbers have dwindled through migration and the synagogue at Cochin has not had a rabbi in living memory. Indian Jews observe the dietary restrictions of the Old Testament, including the ban on pork and the injunction to eat kosher meat. Orthodox Jews eat meat and dairy products in separate meals, even using different pans for each.

The Parsees, the Zoroastrians of Persia, arrived in the 8th century A.D. in Gujarat, in the far west, spreading later to Bombay. They

North India

In the north is the Hindu holy city of Benaras, the city of Lord Shiva, one of the supreme Gods of the holy Hindu trinity. Shiva's consort is Annapoorna, the goddess of food. Food acquires great ritual significance in a Hindu's life: at birth, an infant's head is rubbed with ghee; six months later comes the ritual of Annaprasna when a baby tastes his first solid food; sweets are auspicious so boxes of sweetmeats are exchanged on happy occasions such as festivals, births, and marriages; widows are forbidden from eating "heating" foods such as onions and garlic, also shunned by some ascetics. Even the soul of the dead receives food offerings, called *pinda-daan*. A Hindu's life is traditionally divided into four stages of learning and knowledge; marriage and parenthood; the beginning of detachment from the world (when one's children are married), leading to total renunciation, and there is food prescribed for each stage. Throughout life, the stomach should only be half full of food, leaving it half empty, a quarter for water and a quarter for the movement of air to aid digestion.

Each caste, community, and sect of Hinduism has its own food etiquette and taboos, which were partly designed to maintain caste purity, but these are breaking down, particularly in the big cities, as are the distinctly different cuisines of different religious communities. Earlier, people ate only at home; now, hotels and restaurants often serve a homogenized cuisine with some regional specialities.

Benaras lies on the banks of the sacred river Ganges—orthodox Hindus prefer to drink only Ganges water and erstwhile maharajas carried it abroad in large silver urns—and the rich delta yields a cornucopia of grains, vegetables, and fruit, including mangos. At the gates of ancient Benaras lay Sarnath, where the Buddha came to preach his first sermon in the 6th century B.C.

The Buddha preached the Middle Path of nonviolence and compassion, and his injunction against killing any living being gave the impetus to vegetarianism. Three hundred years later, Emperor Ashoka made Buddhism the state religion, banned hunting, and turned vegetarian. The priestly class followed his example and even today the Brahmin caste tends to be vegetarian, whereas lower castes tend to be meateaters.

The inhospitable Thar desert of Rajasthan, in the northwest, challenged man's culinary creativity. Water was scarce, green vegetables rare, imported rice a luxury. The Marwaris of Rajasthan dried *sangri*, a thorny plant, in the sun and the whip-like fronds had to be soaked for several hours before cooking. Potatoes were a rarity, *bajra* the staple grain and dry red chilies from Jaipur freely used. Pickles livened up a limited meal.

The kings of the desert were keen *shikaris* (hunters) and game cooking developed into a fine art. For example, *sule* was made with venison, wild boar, or sand grouse and *khad* was a layered dish, made with chappatis and

meat, originally baked in a hole in the ground with charcoal and hot sand.

Delhi and the Moghuls

The Arabs had long been coming to India in their *dhows* to trade but in 1000 A.D. the first Muslim invader from Afghanistan defeated the northern Hindu king. For almost a thousand years, Delhi was ruled by Muslims—first by sultans of Arab origin and then the Great Moghul emperors. Islam, with its prohibition on pork and emphasis on eating only *jhatka*/kosher meat, had its own impact on India, particularly through Moghlai cuisine.

Babar, a conqueror from near Samarkand, defeated the Muslim sultan of Delhi at the Battle of Panipat in 1526 A.D. and, for the next 300 years, his family ruled north India, first from Agra, location of the famous Taj Mahal, then from Delhi. The Moghuls took their cultural cue from Persia, adding nuts, saffron, and cream to the cuisine that existed in India. The emperors ate only in the harem because of the threat of poisoning. Over a hundred dishes were prepared for the emperor at each meal. Dishes were locked and sealed in the kitchen and the seal broken in the emperor's presence, where a food taster would taste everything. Harem ladies wore the finest clothes and ate exotic food brought from great distances. Abul Fazal, historian of Emperor Akbar's reign, describes the extravagant grocery shopping list and the lavish meals. For example, ducks, waterfowl, and some vegetables came from Kashmir—as did blocks of ice. Sheep, goat and fowl were especially fattened up—fowls were never kept for less than a month before being slaughtered. High standards were kept up even when the emperor was on the move and living in camps.

Apart from the Moghul kingdom, India had several other important Muslim kingdoms, such as Hyderabad, Awadh, and Rampur, although it is Moghlai cuisine that has become internationally popular.

The Punjab

The magnificent maharajas developed their own culinary styles. The Sikh Maharajas of Patiala, in the northern state of Punjab, enjoyed the fine things of life, including wine and food, and their kitchens were famous. Patiala, for example, employed 35 master chefs, each of whom specialized in only one dish, for example potatoes, and they had about 200 assistants. Punjab is the breadbasket of India. Its rich soil, watered by the famous five rivers, yields abundant harvests of wheat and corn, mustard and sugarcane, and a large variety of vegetables. Milk, yogurt, and ghee are consumed in vast quantities. Sikhism was founded in Punjab in the 15th century by Guru Nanak, who preached a quietist, pacifist faith that reconciled the warring religions of Hinduism and Islam. Nine spiritual gurus followed Guru Nanak and it was the tenth Guru Gobind Singh who gave Sikhs their distinct identity. An important aspect of the faith is the free kitchen at the *gurudwara* (Sikh temple) where any one, irrespective of caste or creed, can enjoy a free meal. Wheat halwa called *kadha prashad* is given as blessed food. The use of tobacco is strictly forbidden, as is beef. Sikhs make up about 2 percent of the population and live mainly in Punjab, Haryana and Delhi.

Anglo-India

The last invaders of India—after the Greeks, Turks, Arabs, Moghuls, Portuguese, and French —were the English. They came for spices but saw rich pickings and stayed to take over the empire of the Great Moghuls. At first, Calcutta, in the northeast, was the capital and the existing clubs, the Tollygunge, the Saturday Club, the Calcutta Club, still reek of the Raj. Kippers for breakfast were imported from England but at Christmas pea-fowl was sometimes served in place of turkey. The clubs of the Raj existed in every civil and military station: the Ooty Club is an imposing Regency building, its walls lined with tiger skins, bison heads, and portraits of former viceroys. The Madras Clubhouse is an imposing 18th-century mansion and Bombay's Willingdon Sports Club and the Royal Bombay Yacht Club survive intact. What is striking about the clubs is their Englishness. Menus still offer puddings such as souffles, trifles, and steamed pudding.

The British inspired the ubiquitous cutlet, now to be found on most Indian railway stations and trains. Other British culinary legacies to India are the toast and some desserts, both "nursery" puddings and others. If what they left behind is meager, what they took away with them when they left India in 1947 is a great deal more and makes a far more interesting story.

Today, Indian "curry" has become a British national dish. British housewives can now pick up tandoori dishes, kormas, Goan fish curry, and dozens of other authentic dishes in supermarkets as part of their weekly shopping. Queen Victoria would have approved. She wanted Indian food, but when her Swiss chef

served up an unpalatable mix of curry powder and water, thickened with plenty of flour, the queen revolted. Then she appointed an Indian servant, Abdul Karim, to cook the royal family authentic curries. Karim became her confidante, taught her Hindustani and was known as "The Munshi."

Now the story of Indian food, as colorful as a spice market, as "chat-patta" as a plate of bhel-poori, has grown and grown, becoming a tale told in many tongues across the world's continents.

Menu Planning

Traditional Indian meals combine meats (optional), grains, pulses, vegetables, milk products (yogurt, paneer, etc.), and sweets (dessert) to provide a well balanced diet.

Vegetarian lunch menu

Mulagu-tanni *114*
A coconut and apple flavored chickpea soup

❖ ❖ ❖

Saag paneer *50*
A combination of fresh spinach and paneer with a hint of garlic

Tamatar, phool gobi, muttar che saar *84*
Cauliflower and peas cooked together in a tomato-flavored tangy masala

Madras potato *124*
A fiery potato dish from southern India

Kadhai chholey *53*
Chickpeas tossed in an onion-tomato masala, flavored with a blend of spices

Gucchi pulao *133*
Fragrant basmati rice and morel mushrooms cooked together with aromatic spices

Naan / parantha / chutneys *128–33*
Assorted Indian breads and chutneys

❖ ❖ ❖

Aam phirni *137*
Traditional Indian dessert made with mangos, rice and milk

Seviyan *139*
Fine vermicelli cooked in milk and scented with cardamoms

Nonvegetarian lunch menu

Chicken cafrael *97*
Traditional Goan delicacy of chicken, marinated in a spicy green paste and then deep-fried

❖ ❖ ❖

Jheenga charchari *66*
A delicacy from Calcutta . . . shrimp stir-fried in pickling spices and garlic

Nilgiri korma *116*
Lamb simmered in a gravy made of fresh greens and flavored with home-made spice mixture

Vanghi *87*
Baby eggplants cooked in a paste made with jaggery, onions and tamarind and spiced with "goda masala"

Sambhar *119*
A south Indian lentil dal with fresh vegetables

Sesame rice *123*
Sesame-flavored basmati rice

Naan / parantha / chutneys *128–33*
Assorted Indian breads and chutneys

❖ ❖ ❖

Kheer *137*
A light dessert made with basmati rice, milk and nuts

Shrikhand *135*
An unusual dessert, made with drained yogurt, sugar, and green cardamom, garnished with nuts

Vegetarian dinner menu

Thakkali rassam *115*

*Essence of tomatoes, enhanced with asafoetida, curry leaves,
and crushed black pepper*

❖ ❖ ❖

Subz kebab *62*

*Seasonal vegetables marinated, grilled, and served
on a skewer*

❖ ❖ ❖

Shobjee jhalfarezi *75*

*Assorted vegetables stir-fried in pickling spices
and coconut*

Baghare baingan *109*

*A Hyderabadi speciality of eggplant cooked
in a gravy made of roasted onions, sesame seeds, jaggery
and coconut*

Rajma *34*

Red kidney beans, Kashmiri style, with ginger and yogurt

Saag dal *111*

*A delicious combination of baby spinach and gram lentils
with a hint of lemon juice*

Tarkari biryani *46*

Fresh seasonal vegetables cooked with fragrant basmati rice

Poori / parantha / naan / roti / chutneys

128–33

Assorted Indian breads and chutneys

❖ ❖ ❖

Kheer *137*

A light dessert made with basmati rice, milk, and nuts

Shahi tukra *139*

*Dessert for royalty . . . deep fried bread soaked in
perfumed milk and covered with reduced milk*

Nonvegetarian dinner menu

Murg shorba *40*

Chicken soup flavored with onion, cumin seeds, and garlic

❖ ❖ ❖

Achari bateyr *49*

Quails cooked in a onion-tomato masala

❖ ❖ ❖

Shrimp balchao *99*

*A Goan speciality of shrimp in a fiery tomato masala with
black pepper, cloves, cinnamon, and fennel*

Dum ka murg *47*

Chicken delicacy cooked in a sealed vessel with mild spices

Dum aloo *36*

*A Kashmiri speciality of potatoes simmered in yogurt
and spices*

Tamatar, phool gobi, muttar che saar *84*

Cauliflower and peas in a tomato-flavored tangy masala

Cabbage poriyal *124*

*Shredded cabbage stir-fried with coconut, mustard seeds,
green coriander, lemon, garlic, and crisp-fried lentil*

Lamb biryani *52*

Lamb cooked with fragrant basmati rice and aromatic spices

Poori / parantha / naan / roti / chutneys

128–33

Assorted Indian breads and chutneys

❖ ❖ ❖

Aam phirni *137*

Traditional Indian dessert made with mangos, rice, and milk

Shahi tukra *139*

*Dessert for the royalty . . . deep fried bread soaked in
perfumed milk and covered with reduced milk*

Flavors
and Textures

Capturing the flavors and textures of Indian food is as complex as trying to describe the myriad patterns and weaves of regional saris, because dishes too vary in appearance, texture, and taste from region to region.

North Indian Punjabi curries are traditionally rich in texture and heavy with ghee, butter, or cream, because that is needed to withstand the cold North Indian winters. Vegetables, too, are slow-cooked in thick onion-based gravy. *Mattar paneer*, for example, is a rich dish of fried cottage cheese cooked with peas in a curry of onions, tomatoes, and spices, with a dash of yogurt. Cooking time is long so that flavors are released slowly.

Thick curries go well with Indian bread such as wheat *chappatis*, *pooris*, *kulchas*, *naan*, and tandoori *roti*. Dry-roasted tandoori meat is marinated for at least six hours before cooking. The tandoor provides wrap-around heat, one of the most effective ways of roasting, and it gives the meat the familiar smoked charcoal flavor.

Bengalis, on the other hand, tend to cook thin fish curries that are more suitable for eating with rice. The popular mustard oil gives dishes a sharp flavor but food is not highly spiced and fresh ginger is widely used. Further northeast, in Assam and Darjeeling, food is often steamed, and some of the world's best tea comes from the great estates there.

The flavors of the desert are robust and food is hot, using the dry red chilies of Jasdan. Game is cooked on open spits or, in parts of Rajasthan, raw meat with whole spices is buried in containers in the hot sand to cook in natural heat, becoming so tender that the meat comes off the bone.

Gujaratis tend to add some sugar to most dishes and they make heavy use of the *sil-batta* (grinding stone) to make masala paste for cooking or for making the legion of fresh chutneys they serve with snacks.

A good tip is to use masala as fresh as possible. Stale garam masala, for example, will not have much flavor, and it is important to use fresh ginger, garlic, and green coriander. The sequential steps in cooking Indian food are vital and should be followed as given in the recipe. Dry spices burn easily and, if this happens, it is better to throw away a batch and start again rather than risk ruining the dish.

It is important to understand spices and their use. Asafoetida, for example, can be used in place of garlic. Inept cooks confuse the palate with dishes that taste of everything all at once, but master chefs use spices skilfully to give each dish a particular flavor. For example, if the dominant note is of green cardamom, then the rest of the spices are subdued and only those are used that complement that particular flavor.

Herbs and Spices

Herbs and spices should be used to heighten the taste and flavor of the main ingredient in a recipe and should never be overpowering. Use only the freshest herbs, and grind spices as you need them—they soon lose their flavor once ground.

1 Dried red chilies
2 Fresh chilies
3 Bay leaves
4 Fresh coriander leaves
5 Curry leaves
6 Stone flower (lichen)
7 Vetiver roots
8 Cinnamon (cassia) bark

9 Nigella seeds
10 Cloves
11 Ground ginger
12 Turmeric
13 Cumin seeds
14 Fennel seeds
15 Coriander seeds
16 Saffron strands
17 Garlic
18 Green cardamom pods
19 Fresh ginger

Pulses and Grains

1

India is predominantly a vegetarian nation, and pulses and grains are, therefore, an important element of the cuisine. The variety grown is astounding, and many are used fresh, rather than the dried varieties we are used to in this country.

3

2

4

1 Brown rice
2 Basmati rice
3 Goan red rice
4 Yellow split peas *(chana dal)*
5 Mung split lentils

5

6   Red chori lentils
7   Green mung beans
8   Urad whole or black lentils
9   Green lentils
10 Shelled urad lentils
11 Red kidney beans
12 Whole brown lentils *(urad dal)*
13 Split red lentils

Basics of Indian Cooking

These basic mixtures are used time and again in Indian cookery. If necessary, increase the quantities given below as specified in individual recipes.

Ginger Paste

Put 2 oz peeled and chopped ginger in a blender or food processor with 1 tablespoon of water and process to a smooth paste. It will keep in the refrigerator for 2–3 days.

Garlic Paste

Put 2 oz peeled and chopped garlic in a blender or food processor with 1 tablespoon of water and process to a smooth paste. It will keep in the refrigerator for 2–3 days.

Green Chili Paste

Put 2 oz green chilies in a blender or food processor with 1 tablespoon of water and process to a smooth paste. It will keep in the refrigerator for 2–3 days.

Raw Onion Paste

Put 2 oz peeled and chopped raw onion in a blender or food processor with 1 tablespoon of water and process to a smooth paste. It will keep in the refrigerator for 2–3 days.

Fried Onion Paste

Deep-fry thinly sliced onions in moderately hot oil until they turn golden brown. Drain on kitchen paper to absorb excess oil. Put the fried onions in a blender or food processor with an equal volume of water and process to a smooth paste. It will keep in the refrigerator for about one week. Alternatively, the fried onions can be stored in an airtight container in the refrigerator, and the paste can be made as and when required.

Cashew Nut Paste

Put 2 oz cashew nuts in a blender or food processor with 4 tablespoons of water and process to a fine paste. It will keep in the refrigerator for 2–3 days.

Ghee

Put 3½ cups heavy cream in a heavy-based pan and bring to the boil. Simmer for about 25 minutes, until all the moisture has evaporated, stirring frequently to prevent sticking. Once all the moisture has evaporated, the mixture should become clear. Stop stirring and let the sediment settle at the bottom, but don't let it burn. Remove from the heat and leave for 5 minutes, then strain through a cheesecloth-lined sieve.

Clarified Butter

Melt 9 oz unsalted butter in a heavy-based pan, then heat over a very low heat for about 10 minutes, until all the froth has settled and the butter becomes clear. Remove from the heat and leave for 3–5 minutes to allow the sediment to settle. Skim any impurities from the top, then gently pour off the clarified butter, leaving the sediment in the base of the pan.

Curry Powder

2 tablespoons ground turmeric
2 tablespoons ground cumin
1 tablespoon red chili powder
4 tablespoons ground coriander
$^{1}/_{2}$ teaspoon asafoetida
$^{1}/_{4}$ teaspoon ground fenugreek seeds

1 Mix all the spices together and store in an airtight container in a cool, dry place. The curry powder will keep for up to a month.

Chat Masala Powder

This is a proprietary spice mixture, available at Indian stores. It is a tangy, spicy, slightly sweet and salty blend of spices that is used to sprinkle onto the finished dish (especially dry dishes), or sometimes included in the dish. Common ingredients are dried ginger, black salt, carom seed, black pepper, black cardamom, green cardamom, cumin, dried mint, fenugreek leaves, dried mango, asafoetida, red chili, and cloves.

Always use fresh herb or vegetable paste immediately after grinding to obtain maximum flavor.

Masalas, as these mixes are known, are always made in different ways, every person making their own particular blend of spices. Use within 2 weeks for maximum flavor.

Garam Masala

¾ oz green cardamom pods
1 oz black cardamom pods
1½ teaspoons cloves
7 cinnamon sticks
  (1 inch long)
5 bay leaves

2 mace blades
1 oz black peppercorns
1 oz cumin seeds
1 oz coriander seeds
½ oz fennel seeds
½ nutmeg

1 Dry-roast all the spices except the nutmeg in a heavy-based frying pan over medium heat for 10 minutes.

2 Grind them in a spice grinder, then grate in the nutmeg, and leave to cool. Store in an airtight container in a cool, dry place.

Chholey Masala

2 oz coriander seeds
2 oz dried mango powder
2 teaspoons black salt
½ oz dried pomegranate
  seeds
10 dried red chilies
½ oz cumin seeds
½ oz green cardamom pods
1 teaspoon black peppercorns
4–5 fenugreek seeds

¼ teaspoon cloves
¼ teaspoon cassia buds
6–8 cinnamon sticks
a pinch of carom seeds
a pinch of freshly grated
  nutmeg
½ teaspoon ground ginger
a pinch of ground mace

1 Dry-roast all the ingredients except the nutmeg, ginger, and mace in a heavy-based frying pan over a low heat for 10–15 minutes.

2 Grind in a spice grinder, then stir in the nutmeg, ginger, and mace and leave to cool. Store in an airtight container in a cool, dry place.

Goda Masala

This blend of spices is used in western India. It should be stirred in toward the end of cooking, as all the spices are already roasted. If it is added at the beginning, not only will it lose its flavor but it will make the dish black in appearance.

1 Dry-roast the first 10 ingredients in a heavy-based pan over low heat for 10–15 minutes, until they give off their aroma. Remove from the pan and set aside. Dry-roast the coconut until golden.

2 Put the coconut and roasted spices in a spice grinder and grind to a fine powder, then stir in the turmeric, asafoetida, and stoneflower. Leave to cool.

3 Store in an airtight container in a cool, dry place.

2 oz coriander seeds
1 teaspoon cumin seeds
½ teaspoon black cumin seeds
⅓ teaspoon black peppercorns
2–3 dried red chilies
5–6 cloves
1 cinnamon stick
2 bay leaves
2 tablespoons sesame seeds
⅓ teaspoon cassia buds
3 tablespoons desiccated
  coconut
½ teaspoon ground turmeric
a pinch of asafoetida
a pinch of stoneflower

Sambhar Powder

This blend of spices is used in southern Indian cooking and varies from region to region.

1 tablespoon peanut oil
1¹/₂ teaspoons channa dal
  (yellow split peas)
1¹/₂ teaspoons urad dal *(black*
  gram beans)
1 tablespoon coriander seeds
2 teaspoons cumin seeds

1 teaspoon black peppercorns
1 teaspoon mustard seeds
1 teaspoon fenugreek seeds
3 dried red chilies
¹/₂ teaspoon ground turmeric
a generous pinch of
  asafoetida

1 Heat the oil in a frying pan, add the *channa dal* and *urad dal* and fry over a low heat until they turn golden brown. Remove from the pan and drain on paper toweling to absorb excess oil.

2 Put all the ingredients, including the dal, into a spice grinder and grind to a fine powder. Store in an airtight container in a cool, dry place.

Achari or Panch Phoran Spice Mix

This spice mix can be used whole for tempering or ground and stored in an airtight container.

1 oz cumin seeds
4 oz anise seeds
2 oz mustard seeds

¹/₂ teaspoon fenugreek seeds
¹/₂ teaspoon onion seeds
  (nigella seeds)

1 To use the spice mix whole, simply mix all the spices together.

2 For a ground spice mix, dry-roast the spices in a heavy-based frying pan over a low heat for 10–15 minutes. Grind them in a spice grinder and leave to cool. Store in an airtight container in a cool, dry place.

Boondi

This is made from chickpea flour and is usually available in Indian shops. Here's how to make your own.

11 oz chickpea flour
a pinch of ground turmeric
¹/₄ teaspoon ground cumin
a pinch of asafoetida

a pinch of baking powder
2 cups plus 2 tablespoons oil
  for deep-frying
salt to taste

1 Put all the ingredients except the oil in a bowl, add 3 tablespoons of water, and mix together to make a batter. It should have a coating consistency and should not be too thin. Set aside for 30 minutes.

2 Heat the oil over a medium heat. Pour in a little of the batter through a perforated spoon so that it falls into the pan in droplets.

3 Remove the fried balls from the oil just before they start to turn golden brown and drain on paper toweling. Repeat with the remaining batter. Store in an airtight container in a cool, dry place.

A typical Kashmiri Muslim feast is called a *Wazwan*—a highly formal meal that consists of 36 courses, of which at least half are meat dishes.

Kashmir

The Moghul Emperor Jahangir said of Kashmir, "If there is paradise on earth, it is here, it is here, it is here!" The valley of Kashmir, ringed by majestic Himalayan mountains, home to the mountain antelope whose wool is made into the famous pashmina shawls, is a sylvan land of lakes, trees, and gardens. Almond trees blossom in March, the chinar is in leaf in April, strawberries and cherries abound in May, and apricots follow in June. Autumn brings pears and pomegranates. No wonder Jahangir exclaimed, "*Gar firdaus baruae zami ast; Hamee ast, hamee ast, hamee ast!*"

Like the rest of India, Kashmir has a mixed religious pedigree. Both Buddhism and Hinduism flourished there and Islam arrived in the 14th century, almost two hundred years before Kashmir was conquered by the Moghul Emperor Akbar. Before the advent of Islam, pork was widely eaten. Later, Kashmiri Hindus adopted many elements of Moghul cooking. Brahmins, for example, are generally vegetarian but many Kashmiri Brahmins became meateaters. There are some basic differences between the cuisine of Hindu Kashmiri Pandits and Kashmiri Muslims—for example, Hindus generally use yogurt and *hing* (asafoetida) to flavor their food while Muslims use onions and garlic. For Hindus, one of the most important festivals is Shivratri, the festival of Lord Shiva, when families both pray and feast together. Navreh, the Kashmiri new year, is welcomed with a *thaali* piled with rice, yogurt, honey, walnuts, and other symbols of prosperity.

Kashmiris use a number of dried vegetables in their cooking, such as turnips, tomatoes, beans, peas, and cabbage, grown in summer on the lakes and dried for use in the long, harsh winters when the valley is snowbound, temperatures drop to about 20 degrees Fahrenheit, and Kashmiris carry around individual charcoal fires for warmth. Hot *kahwah*—green tea brewed in samovars with cardamom and almonds—is sipped all day long. Saffron was introduced to Kashmir from Mediterranean countries and is widely used in cooking. Nuts and dried fruit are popular in winter, and both rice and wheat are staples: rice is cooked in many forms, both savory and sweet; and many types of wheat bread are eaten, such as *kulchas*, *sheermal*, and the soft *bakarkhani*.

The Kashmiris eat seated on the floor—as is the custom in India. A piece of cloth called *dastarkhwan* is put on the floor and the food placed on it; people sit around the cloth and eat from plates called *trami*. Each *trami* can hold enough food for 3–4 people, and that is how the food is eaten—by sharing.

Qalia means gravy with the ingredients blended with water.

It is a general term for a lamb or chicken dish in Kashmir.

Qalia

Lamb chops in yogurt gravy

1 Heat the ghee or clarified butter in a large pan. Add the asafoetida, yogurt, cloves, lamb, chili powder, ginger paste, ground ginger, ground fennel seed, and some salt. Simmer, uncovered, for 20 minutes, letting the juices from the meat and yoghurt evaporate until a reddish-brown sediment appears. Stir frequently to prevent burning.

2 Scrape up the sediment from the base of the pan, turning the meat frequently until it is brown. Add slightly less than 7 tablespoons water and cook for 10–15 minutes.

3 Add the turmeric and stir it in well. Add 1 cup water and simmer for 15 minutes.

4 Add the potatoes and another 7 tablespoons water, then cover and cook until the meat is tender. The sauce should be thin but not watery.

5 Stir in the garam masala, sugar, and chopped fresh coriander.

Serves 4–6

$^1/_2$ cup ghee or clarified butter
  (see page 23)
$^1/_8$ teaspoon asafoetida
7 oz yogurt, preferably Greek
  yogurt, whisked
4 cloves
$2^1/_4$ lb double lamb chops (i.e.,
  2 chops joined together)
1 teaspoon red chili powder
1 tablespoon Ginger Paste
  (see page 22)
$^1/_8$ teaspoon ground ginger
$^1/_4$ teaspoon ground fennel
  seed
salt to taste
2 teaspoons ground turmeric
9 oz potatoes, peeled and cut
  into 1-inch cubes
1 teaspoon Garam Masala
  (see page 24)
1 tablespoon sugar
4 tablespoons chopped fresh
  coriander
salt to taste

Qalia originated in snowbound areas where, to keep the cold at bay, warm liquids were needed; this soupy dish could be eaten as well as drunk.

Roganjosh is a derivative of *Rogangosht*,

literally meaning lamb curry with saffron-infused oil.

Roganjosh

Lamb curry

Serves 4–6

1/2 cup vegetable oil

4 cloves

3 cinnamon sticks

1/4 teaspoon asafoetida

2 1/4 lb boneless leg of lamb,
  cut into 1-inch dice

10 oz yogurt, preferably
  Greek yogurt, whisked

2 tablespoons Ginger Paste
  (see page 22)

1 tablespoon red chili powder

1/2 teaspoon ground ginger

1 tablespoon sugar

salt to taste

1 teaspoon Garam Masala
  (see page 24)

1/4 teaspoon saffron strands

4 tablespoons khoya (reduced
  milk) or whole milk powder

1 oz ground almonds

1/2 teaspoon bottled vetiver
  water

1 tablespoon finely shredded
  fresh ginger

2 tablespoons fresh coriander
  leaves

1 Heat the oil in a large pan, add the whole spices, asafoetida, lamb, yogurt, ginger paste, chili powder, and ground ginger. Cover and simmer over a very low heat for 20–25 minutes, until all the juices from the meat and yogurt evaporate and a reddish-brown sediment begins to appear.

2 Scrape up the sediment from the base of the pan and continue to cook, turning the meat, for about 15 minutes, until the meat turns reddish brown.

3 Add the sugar and some salt to taste, then pour in 1/2 cup water. Cover and cook over a very low heat for 20 minutes. Add the garam masala and saffron and cook for another 5 minutes.

4 When the meat is nearly done, add the *khoya* or milk powder and ground almonds. Cook gently for another 10 minutes, until most of the liquid has been absorbed. Sprinkle over the vetiver water and garnish with the shredded ginger and coriander leaves.

Shab means night and *degh* is the cooking vessel.

As the name suggests, this dish is traditionally cooked overnight.

Shabdegh

Lamb with chili, ginger, and turnips

1 Heat the ghee or clarified butter in a large pan, add the asafoetida, cloves, lamb, chili powder, and some salt and fry until reddish-brown, sprinkling in about a tablespoon of water to prevent burning.

2 Tie up the ground fennel seed and garam masala spices in a piece of cheesecloth and add to the pan with the turmeric, ginger paste and yogurt. Pour in 3½ cups water, cover, and simmer over very low heat for at least 2–3 hours. If the mixture becomes too dry, add a couple of tablespoons of water from time to time.

3 When the meat becomes soft and starts to stick to the fingers, add the turnips and sugar and cook for another 30 minutes.

4 At the end of cooking there should be only a little liquid left. Remove the cheesecloth bag and garnish with the chopped fresh coriander.

Serves 4–6

1 cup minus 2 tablespoons ghee or clarified butter (see page 23)
¼ teaspoon asafoetida
4 cloves
2¼ lb shoulder of lamb, cut into large cubes on the bone (ask your butcher to do this)
1 teaspoon red chili powder
salt to taste
1 teaspoon ground fennel seed
1 teaspoon whole Garam Masala spices (see page 24), made to step 1
1½ teaspoons ground turmeric
2 tablespoons Ginger Paste (see page 22)
1 cup minus 2 tablespoons yogurt, preferably Greek yogurt, whisked
1 lb 2 oz turnips, peeled and quartered
1 teaspoon sugar
a bunch of fresh coriander, chopped

Serve *Khurmani Ka Murg* with *Gucchi Pulao* (see below). Fried onions, which are used to garnish this dish, are available ready cooked in supermarkets and Indian stores.

Khurmani Ka Murg

Chicken with apricots

1 Soak the dried apricots in hot water until softened. Heat the ghee or clarified butter in a large pan and add the yogurt. Stir for 10 minutes, until the yogurt turns brown, then add the apricots and cook, stirring, for 5 minutes.

2 Add the chicken pieces to the pan and cook, stirring, for 5 minutes, until lightly colored. Add all the remaining ingredients except the thinly sliced almonds, then pour in 1¾ cups water and bring to a boil.

3 Simmer for 20 minutes, until the chicken is tender. Garnish with the thinly sliced almonds.

Serves 4–6

4 oz dried apricots
2 tablespoons ghee or clarified butter (see page 23)
½ cup yogurt, preferably Greek yogurt, whisked
8 chicken pieces, skinned (weighing about 2¼ lb)
4 teaspoons ground fennel seed
2 teaspoons ground ginger
1 teaspoon ground cinnamon
½ teaspoon cumin seeds
4 green cardamom pods
½ teaspoon red chili powder
4 tablespoons Fried Onion Paste (see page 23)
4 tablespoons blanched almonds, halved
fried onions
salt to taste
1 tablespoon thinly sliced almonds

Gucchi Pulao

Mushroom pilaf

1 Strain the mushroom soaking water and reserve. Clean the morels thoroughly in cold running water, then drain.

2 Heat half the clarified butter or oil in a pan, add the morels and fry for 2–3 minutes. Add the salt and ⅞ cup water and cook for another 5–7 minutes, until the morels are tender and have absorbed the water. Remove from the heat and set aside.

3 In a separate pan, heat the remaining clarified butter or oil and add the whole spices and bay leaf. Fry until they begin to splutter, then add the onion, ginger, chili and yogurt, and fry until golden brown. Add the rice, the morel soaking liquid and 1¼ cups water and bring to a boil. Reduce the heat to very low and cook, covered, for 20–25 minutes, until the rice is tender.

4 Mix the morels into the rice and continue cooking until there is no moisture left. Leave over a very low heat or on a hot plate for 5 minutes. Then garnish with the almonds, pistachios, cashew nuts, and the lime zest and serve.

Serves 4–6

¼ oz dried morel mushrooms, soaked in 4 tablespoons of boiling water for 30 minutes, drained (water reserved) and cut in half lengthways
4 tablespoons clarified butter (see page 23) or vegetable oil
1 teaspoon salt
1 cinnamon stick
3 cloves
3 green cardamom pods
1 bay leaf
1 tablespoon very finely chopped onion
1 teaspoon very finely chopped fresh ginger
1 green chili, cut in half
1 tablespoon yogurt, preferably Greek yogurt, whisked
9 oz basmati rice
1 tablespoon each almonds, pistachios, and cashew nuts
finely chopped zest of 1 lime

When kidney beans are fully cooked, the skins will be cracked or peeling, not intact.

When pressed the beans must be soft.

Rajma

Spiced kidney beans

1 Drain the soaked beans, then put them in a pan and add double the volume of water. Add the turmeric, ground fennel seed, ginger, bay leaves, and some salt, bring to a boil and boil hard for 10 minutes. Reduce the heat to low and simmer until the beans are tender.

2 Heat the ghee or oil in a separate pan. Add the asafoetida, cumin seeds, chili powder, and green chili paste. Cook until they start to splutter, then add them to the beans.

3 Add the ground pomegranate seeds (or lemon juice) and garam masala and simmer for 5 minutes. Garnish with the fresh coriander leaves and strips of ginger before serving.

Serves 4–6

9 oz dried red kidney beans, soaked in cold water overnight
½ teaspoon ground turmeric
1 tablespoon ground fennel seed
½ tablespoon ground ginger
3 bay leaves
salt to taste
2 tablespoons ghee (see page 23) or vegetable oil
¼ teaspoon asafoetida
1 teaspoon cumin seeds
1 teaspoon red chili powder
1 teaspoon Green Chili Paste (see page 22)
1 teaspoon ground pomegranate seeds (or 1 tablespoon lemon juice)
1 teaspoon Garam Masala (see page 24)
¾ oz fresh coriander leaves
large knob of fresh ginger, cut into julienne strips

Red kidney beans are best enjoyed when freshly picked from the plant; then they just need steaming and are simply irresistible. The more common dried version needs soaking.

There are a lot of variations on this famous dish. Vegetables such as okra,

jackfruit, and colcasia can be cooked with the potatoes in the same manner.

Dum Aloo

Whole spiced potatoes

1 Peel the potatoes and prick them all over with a fork. In a deep pan, heat the mustard oil to smoking point, then deep-fry the potatoes in it until golden brown. Remove and set aside.

2 Heat a little of the same oil in a separate pan, add the cloves, cumin, and asafoetida and fry until they start to splutter.

3 Add the potatoes, chili powder, coriander, salt and 1¾ cup water. Bring to a boil and cook for 5 minutes, then stir in the ginger paste, shredded ginger, and sugar and cook for 5 minutes more.

4 Add the yogurt and cook on a low heat for 10 minutes. Sprinkle with the garam masala and serve.

Serves 4–6

2¼ lb baby new potatoes
8 fl oz mustard oil
4 cloves
½ teaspoon cumin seeds
¼ teaspoon asafoetida
½ teaspoon red chili powder
1 teaspoon ground coriander
salt to taste
1 teaspoon Ginger Paste (see page 24)
1 tablespoon finely shredded fresh ginger
1 teaspoon sugar
½ cup yogurt, preferably Greek yoghurt, whisked
1 tablespoon Garam Masala (see page 24)

Karamkalla

Stir-fried spiced cabbage

Serves 4–6

3½ fl oz mustard oil

¼ teaspoon asafoetida

½ teaspoon cumin seeds

a pinch of fenugreek seeds

1 teaspoon Ginger Paste (see
page 22)

1 teaspoon finely chopped
green chili

½ teaspoon ground ginger

1 large white or green cabbage
(not Savoy), cut into 4-inch
pieces

½ teaspoon red chili powder

a generous pinch of Garam
Masala (see page 24)

1 teaspoon sugar

a pinch of ground turmeric

½ teaspoon ground coriander

salt to taste

1 tablespoon chopped fresh
coriander

1 In a large pan, heat the oil to smoking point, then add the asafoetida, cumin seeds, fenugreek seeds, ginger paste, green chili, and ground ginger.

2 Immediately add the cabbage, chilli powder, garam masala, sugar, ground turmeric, ground coriander, and some salt and stir until well mixed.

3 Add 2 tablespoons of water and cook, uncovered, over a medium heat for about 15 minutes, or until the cabbage is tender and there is no liquid left. Add the chopped fresh coriander and toss well before serving.

The Moghlai style of cooking was adopted by several maharajas and nawabs, most notably the rulers of Hyderabad, Awadh, Rampur, and Patiala.

Moghlai

The Great Moghuls, probably history's grandest dynasty, were epicures. Moghul style blossomed in the 16th century, in the reign of the third emperor, Akbar, a period of great stability. Family life was based in the harem, where the emperor ate all his meals. The harem was a city in itself, with 5,000 members at its zenith, including princesses, amazonian guards, and eunuchs. Vast quantities of exquisite food, dried and fresh fruit such as mangos, melons, grapes, peaches, pomegranates, pineapple, and custard apple, brought from Kashmir, Kabul, Samarkand, and Kandahar, were consumed. A contemporary European traveller wrote that Moghul ladies drank a great deal of expensive wine from Shiraz, a habit acquired from their husbands. Abul Fazal, the historian of Emperor Akbar's reign, wrote of the imperial kitchens: "Cooks from all countries prepare a great variety of dishes of all kinds of grains, greens, meats; also oily, sweet, and spicy dishes. The victuals are served in dishes of gold and silver, stone and earthenware. Some victuals are also kept half-ready so that in the space of an hour a hundred dishes are served up." Despite these elaborate preparations, Akbar ate lightly and only once a day, abstained from eating meat on several days, including Fridays and in November, his birth month, and drank only pure Ganges water—he called it the "water of immortality."

Akbar's son, Jahangir, describes fantastic parties arranged for him by favorite queens. A single dinner, for example, hosted by Empress Noor Jahan in 1617 to celebrate a great military victory, cost her Rs.300,000, equivalent to about $4.2 million today. Incidentally, Jahangir's son, Emperor Shahjahan, built the wondrous Taj Mahal.

Scholars argue that the nomadic and barbaric Moghuls, descendants of Mongols, could not have created a distinctive cuisine before they settled in India. Moghul emperors, however, took what they found in India, notably the food of the Hindu *kayast* kitchens, added nuts, saffron, and cream to create fusion cuisine now called Moghlai. Tomatoes, brought to India by the Portuguese, were first used by Empress Noor Jahan with browned onions to create the moghul curry sauce. The anglicized word "curry," derived from the Tamil word *kari* or sauce, describes an aromatized stew simmered in water in a heavy pan over gentle heat that helps to blend the flavors.

The internationally popular Moghlai food today is a lighter version of food made for the emperors, substituting oil for ghee and using less cream and nuts.

A very effective soup for helping the system to fight cold, and strengthen the bones. It provides energy and keeps you warm in winter.

Murg Shorba

Chicken and yogurt soup

Serves 4–6

2¼ lb raw chicken bones
6 tablespoons vegetable oil
5 oz red onions, finely
   chopped
9 oz tomatoes, finely chopped
9 oz yogurt, preferably Greek
   yogurt, whisked
3 green chilies (left whole)
2 tablespoons crushed garlic
1 tablespoon finely chopped
   fresh ginger
1 tablespoon chopped fresh
   mint
2 teaspoons ground coriander
1 teaspoon Garam Masala
   (see page 24)
½ teaspoon ground turmeric
1 teaspoon red chili powder
1 teaspoon cumin seeds, dry-
   roasted in a frying pan and
   then ground
salt to taste
2 teaspoons finely chopped
   fresh coriander
shredded cooked chicken, to
   garnish (optional)
julienne strips of tomato

For tempering:

2 teaspoons vegetable oil
1 teaspoon cumin seeds
¼ teaspoon onion seeds
   (nigella seeds)
2 tablespoons gram flour
   (chickpea flour)

1 Bring 8 cups water to a boil in a large pan, add the chicken bones and blanch for 1 minute. Drain and set aside.

2 Heat the oil in a pan, add the onions, and fry until golden brown. Add all the remaining ingredients, except the chicken bones and fresh coriander and stir-fry for 30 seconds.

3 Add the chicken bones and stir-fry for 5 minutes. Then add 3½ quarts water and bring to a boil, skimming off the scum from the surface. Reduce the heat to as low as possible and simmer gently for 45 minutes. Strain the stock through a cheesecloth into a clean pan and bring back to a simmer.

4 Heat the oil for tempering in a small pan. Add the cumin and onion seeds and fry until they start to splutter. Add the gram flour and fry till it turns golden brown. Add this mixture to the chicken stock and simmer for 10 minutes. Garnish with the chopped fresh coriander, cooked chicken strips, if using, and julienne of tomato.

Homemade soups are rarely thick in India. The emphasis is on flavors to rejuvenate the tastebuds, and induce the appetite.

Murg Tikka Masala has always been popular in India, but as a dry dish.

A popular variation is made with added fresh cream to provide the sauce.

Murg Tikka Masala

Chicken tikka masala

Serves 4–6

2¼ lb boneless chicken
 breasts, cut into bite-sized
 pieces

For the marinade:

½ teaspoon Ginger Paste (see
 page 22)

½ teaspoon Garlic Paste (see
 page 22)

1½ teaspoons lemon juice

1 tablespoon vegetable oil

½ cup yogurt, preferably
 Greek yogurt, whisked

1 teaspoon cumin seeds, dry-
 roasted in a frying pan and
 then ground

½ teaspoon red chili powder

salt to taste

For the sauce:

½ cup vegetable oil

1 lb 6oz Raw Onion Paste
 (see page 22)

1 teaspoon Ginger Paste (see
 page 22)

1 teaspoon Garlic Paste (see
 page 22)

1 teaspoon Green Chili Paste
 (see page 22)

1 teaspoon red chili powder

½ teaspoon ground turmeric

1 teaspoon ground coriander

salt to taste

11 oz fresh tomatoes, puréed

3 tablespoons light cream

2 tablespoons chopped fresh
 coriander

¼ teaspoon Garam Masala
 (see page 24)

1 Mix together all the ingredients for the marinade. Add the chicken, making sure it is well coated, and let marinate for 2 hours.

2 Spread the chicken pieces out on a baking tray and bake in an oven preheated to 350°F for 15 minutes (ideally it should be cooked in a tandoor, which is how it is done traditionally).

3 For the sauce, heat the oil in a pan, add the onion paste and cook, stirring, until it is golden brown. Add the ginger, garlic, and green chili pastes and stir-fry for 2 minutes. Add the ground spices and salt and stir-fry for 30 seconds. Add 1 cup water and the puréed tomatoes and cook for 12–15 minutes, or until the mixture has the consistency of heavy cream.

4 Add the chicken pieces to the sauce and cook for 5–8 minutes. Stir in the cream and chopped coriander, then sprinkle over the garam masala.

Marinate and cook the chicken as for *Murg Tikka Masala*

(opposite) but serve with the following sauces:

Murg Mumtaz

Chicken in tomato, fenugreek, and almond gravy

1 Prepare the chicken as on page 42 to the end of step 2. For the sauce, put the puréed tomatoes, ginger, garlicand green chili pastes, and ground spices in a pan with 2 cups plus 2 tablespoons water and bring to a boil. Cook for 30 minutes, then strain through a sieve into a clean pan. Simmer for 10 minutes more.

2 Put the almonds in a blender with 1 cup water and blend to a smooth paste. Add to the pan with all the remaining ingredients and the chicken tikka and cook for 10 minutes.

Serves 4–6

chicken and marinade as for
  Chicken Tikka Masala (see
  page 42)
2 ¼ lb fresh tomatoes, puréed
½ teaspoon Ginger Paste (see
  page 22)
1 teaspoon Garlic Paste (see
  page 22)
½ teaspoon Green Chili Paste
  (see page 22)
1 teaspoon red chili powder
½ teaspoon ground cloves

1 teaspoon ground green
  cardamom
7 oz thinly sliced almonds
7 oz butter
½ cup light cream
2 teaspoons ground fenugreek
  leaves
1 teaspoon Garam Masala
  (see page 24)
salt to taste

Murg Makhani

Butter chicken

1 Prepare the chicken as on page 42 to the end of step 2. For the sauce, put the puréed tomatoes, ginger, garlic, and green chili pastes, chili powder, crushed peppercorns, coriander stalks, bay leaves, cloves, and cardamom in a pan with 2 cups plus 2 tablespoons water and salt to taste. Bring to a boil and cook for 30 minutes.

2 Strain the mixture through a fine sieve into a clean pan and simmer for 10 minutes. Add all the remaining ingredients and the chicken tikka and simmer for a further 10 minutes, until the sauce is the consistency of heavy cream.

Serves 4–6

chicken and marinade as for
  Chicken Tikka Masala (see
  page 42)
2 ¼ lb fresh tomatoes, puréed
1 teaspoon Ginger Paste (see
  page 22)
1 teaspoon Garlic Paste (see
  page 22)
½ teaspoon Green Chili Paste
  (see page 22)
½ teaspoon red chili powder
½ teaspoon black
  peppercorns, crushed
2 teaspoons chopped fresh
  coriander stalks

2–3 bay leaves
a pinch of ground cloves
½ teaspoon ground green
  cardamom
3 tablespoons butter
7 tablespoons light cream
½ teaspoon ground fenugreek
a pinch of Garam Masala (see
  page 24)
1 tablespoon granulated sugar
salt to taste

Moghlai dishes are all derived from the royal kitchens of the Moghuls. The rich and delicate flavors are a revelation.

Traditionally, meat was beaten with spices and fat into smaller pieces on a stone slab to keep the meat cold and ensure tenderness.

Badami Kofta

Lamb meatballs with almonds

1 For the meatballs, mix everything together except the almonds (but including the ice, which keeps the meatballs well chilled) and mince to a very fine paste. Keep in the refrigerator.

2 For the sauce, put the toasted almonds in a blender with 7 tablespoons water and blend to a paste.

3 Heat the ghee or clarified butter in a pan, add the whole spices, and fry until they begin to splutter. Add the puréed onions and cook, stirring, until they turn golden brown. Then add the puréed tomatoes, turmeric, chili powder, garlic, ginger and green chili pastes, and some salt and cook, stirring, for about 15 minutes, until the oil separates from the mixture.

4 Add 2 cups plus 2 tablespoons water, the almond paste, and the sugar and simmer for 30 minutes. Meanwhile, take the meat mixture out of the refrigerator and shape into 24 balls. Stuff each ball with a blanched almond, reshaping if necessary so the almond is completely enclosed.

5 Put the meatballs into the sauce and poach over very low heat for 20 minutes. Drizzle over the cream and chopped fresh coriander.

Serves 4–6

1 lb 5 oz boneless shoulder of lamb, cut into 1-inch cubes
2 oz lamb fat
2 eggs
1 teaspoon ground black cardamom
1½ teaspoons ground green cardamom
½ teaspoon ground cloves
1 teaspoon ground cinnamon
1 tablespoon finely chopped fresh ginger
1 tablespoon chopped fresh coriander stalks
2 oz ice, crushed
salt to taste
24 blanched almonds

For the sauce:

2 oz toasted flaked almonds
4 tablespoons ghee or clarified butter (see page 23)
4 green cardamom pods
2 black cardamom pods
2 cinnamon sticks
7 oz onions, puréed
5 oz fresh tomatoes, puréed
¼ teaspoon ground turmeric
1 teaspoon red chili powder
1 tablespoon Garlic Paste (see page 22)
1 teaspoon Ginger Paste (see page 22)
1 teaspoon Green Chili Paste (see page 22)
salt to taste
1 tablespoon granulated sugar
4 tablespoons light cream
1 tablespoon chopped fresh coriander

Moghlai cooks were very creative, and the inclusions of cream, yogurt and fruits with vegetables are attributed to their expertise.

Tarkari Biryani

Mixed vegetable and cheese biryani

1 Soak the rice in cold water for 1 hour, then drain and parboil 5 pints salted water for 8–10 minutes. Drain off excess water and set aside. Warm the milk, add the saffron and rosewater and set aside for 30 minutes.

2 Heat the ghee or clarified butter in a pan, add the whole spices and fry until they begin to splutter. Add the vegetables, paneer, cashew nuts, raisins, and green chili and stir-fry for 5 minutes.

3 Add the cream and some salt and bring to a boil. Simmer for 5 minutes and then remove from the heat (this is the vegetable curry for the biryani).

4 Layer the rice and vegetable curry in a greased ovenproof dish, sprinkling each layer of vegetable curry with the ground cardamom, mace, and ground fenugreek leaves. There should be at least 3 layers of rice with 2 layers of curry. Pour the saffron mixture over the top.

5 Cover tightly with foil and cook for 1 hour in an oven preheated to 300°F.

Serves 4–6

1lb 5 oz basmati rice
7 tablespoons milk
4 pinches of saffron
2 tablespoons rosewater
7 oz ghee or clarified butter
   (see page 23)
6 green cardamom pods
2 cinnamon sticks
3 bay leaves
5 cloves
2 blades of mace
$^{1}/_{4}$ lb cauliflower florets
$^{1}/_{4}$ lb peas
$^{1}/_{4}$ lb potatoes, peeled and cut
   into $^{1}/_{2}$-inch cubes
$^{1}/_{4}$ lb carrots, peeled and cut
   into $^{1}/_{2}$-inch cubes
$^{1}/_{4}$ lb button mushrooms,
   quartered
$^{1}/_{4}$ lb paneer, cut into $^{1}/_{2}$-inch
   cubes
2 oz cashew nuts
2 oz raisins
1 tablespoon finely chopped
   green chili
$2^{1}/_{2}$ cups light cream
salt to taste
1 oz ground green cardamom
$^{1}/_{2}$ teaspoon ground mace
2 teaspoons ground fenugreek
   leaves

Paneer:

This is an Indian fresh milk cheese made from boiling whole milk, then adding lemon juice or vinegar to form curds. The liquid whey is drained off the curds, which are then pressed and formed into cakes. It is similar to farmer cheese or pot cheese.

Dum is a method of cooking outdoors – to cook the results of a day's hunting—

in stoves dug underground to protect the wood fires from the wind.

Dum Ka Murg

Chicken in onion, yogurt and almond gravy

Serves 4–6

3 tablespoons ghee or clarified
  butter (see page 23)
9 oz onions, sliced
2 oz toasted flaked almonds
1 teaspoon ground coriander
a pinch of ground turmeric
½ teaspoon Garlic Paste (see
  page 22)
9 oz yogurt, preferably Greek
  yogurt, whisked

a pinch of Garam Masala (see
  page 24)
salt to taste
2 ¼ lb boneless chicken
  breasts, cut into bite-sized
  pieces
1 teaspoon tomato purée
toasted cashew nuts
zest of 1 lime

1 Heat the ghee or clarified butter in a pan, add the onions and
sauté until golden brown. Remove the onions from the pan with
a slotted spoon, drain on paper toweling, and purée in a blender
with 7 tablespoons water. Set aside.

2 Put the toasted flaked almonds in a blender with 14
tablespoons water and whizz to a paste, then set aside.

3 Reheat the ghee in which the onions were cooked, add the
coriander, turmeric, garlic paste, yogurt, garam masala, some
salt, and 1³/4 cup water. Cook, stirring, for 5 minutes, until the
mixture acquires a sandy texture.

4 Add the chicken and cook, stirring, for 5 minutes. Finally add
the onion and almond purées and the tomato purée and cook for
10 minutes, until the sauce has a coating consistency. Garnish
with the cashew nuts and lime zest and serve.

Moghuls loved hunting wildfowl and incorporated several aromatic spices in their recipes for cooking it.

Achari Bateyr

Spiced whole quail

Serves 4–6

4 tablespoons mustard oil

¾ teaspoon whole Achari Spice Mix (see page 24)

9 oz onions, chopped

11 oz tomatoes, finely chopped

¾ teaspoon ground Achari Spice Mix (see page 24)

1 teaspoon ground coriander

1 teaspoon ground cumin

1 teaspoon red chili powder

⅓ teaspoon ground turmeric

1 teaspoon dried mango powder

½ teaspoon ground fenugreek leaves

½ teaspoon Ginger Paste (see page 22)

1 teaspoon Garlic Paste (see page 22)

salt to taste

4 quails

1 tablespoon lemon juice

1 teaspoon finely chopped fresh coriander

1 Heat the mustard oil in a large pan, add the whole achari spices, and fry until they begin to splutter. Add the onions and stir-fry until they turn golden brown.

2 Add the tomatoes, all the ground spices, the ginger and garlic pastes and some salt and cook, stirring, for 15 minutes. Add the quails and fry until browned all over.

3 Cover the pan and cook on a very low heat for 15 minutes or until the quails are tender. Stir in the lemon juice and fresh coriander. Serve with *naan* bread.

Venison was the favourite meat of the Moghuls – it was purported to possess aphrodisiac qualities! Serve the venison on a bed of *Saag Paneer* (see below).

Janglee Maans

Venison in spicy sauce

1 Heat the ghee or clarified butter in a pan, add the whole spices, and cook until they begin to splutter. Add the onions and stir-fry until they turn golden brown.

2 Add the venison, the ginger and garlic pastes, chili powder, turmeric, coriander, yogurt and some salt and cook, stirring, over a medium heat for 20 minutes. Add $^1/_2$ cup water and cook for 20 minutes, stirring occasionally.

3 Add 1 cup water, then cover and cook on a very low heat for 25 minutes, until the meat is tender. Stir in the garam masala.

Serves 4–6
5 oz ghee or clarified butter (see page 23)
5–6 dried red chilies
6–8 green cardamom pods
3–4 black cardamom pods
6–8 cloves
7 oz onions, finely chopped
2$^1/_4$ lb boneless venison, cut into 1-inch cubes
1 tablespoon Ginger Paste (see page 22)
2 tablespoons Garlic Paste (see page 22)
1 tablespoon red chili powder
$^1/_2$ teaspoon ground turmeric
1 tablespoon ground coriander
5 oz yogurt, preferably Greek yogurt, whisked
salt to taste
1 teaspoon Garam Masala (see page 24)

Saag Paneer

Spinach and cheese

Serves 4–6
4$^1/_2$ lb fresh spinach, well washed
2 oz ghee or clarified butter (see page 23)
$^1/_2$ teaspoon cumin seeds
2 oz onions, finely chopped
2 oz tomatoes, finely chopped
1 teaspoon Garlic Paste (see page 22)
1 tablespoon finely chopped fresh ginger
$^1/_2$ teaspoon red chili powder
$^1/_2$ teaspoon ground coriander
salt to taste
7 oz paneer, cut into $^1/_2$-inch dice
2 tablespoons light cream
1 teaspoon lemon juice
2 teaspoon chopped fresh coriander

1 Bring a large pan of water to a boil and blanch the spinach leaves. Drain well and refresh in cold water to retain their bright green color. Drain again and then purée, or chop finely, the spinach in a blender.

2 Heat the ghee or clarified butter in a pan, add the cumin seeds, and fry until they begin to splutter. Add the chopped onions and stir-fry until they turn golden brown. Then add the tomatoes, garlic paste, chopped ginger, chili powder, ground coriander and some salt and stir-fry for 2 minutes.

3 Add the diced paneer and stir-fry for 30 seconds. Then add the spinach purée and cook for 3-4 minutes. Stir in the cream, lemon juice, and chopped fresh coriander.

Only the elite could afford to hunt. Once caught, the venison was cooked and consumed in the jungle, using just a few other ingredients carried by the hunters on their trek.

This is a definitive festive celebration dish, with infinite methods of preparation;

all over India people have their own ways of making *biryani*.

Lamb Biryani

Lamb with fragrant basmati rice

1 Heat the ghee or clarified butter in a large pan, add the whole spices, and fry for 10 seconds. Add the lamb and sauté until lightly browned.

2 Add the yogurt, chili powder, ginger paste and asafoetida and cook over a low heat for about 1 hour, until the meat is tender. Stir every 5 minutes to prevent the mixture sticking.
The liquid (the juices from the meat) should become a coating consistency.

3 Stir in all the remaining spices and cook for 5 minutes. Add 1 cup minus 1 tablespoon water, bring to a boil, cook for 5 minutes, and remove from the heat.

4 Parboil the rice with a pinch of salt in 5 cups water for 8–10 minutes. Drain off the excess water and set aside.

5 Warm the milk and add the saffron to it. In a greased ovenproof dish, sprinkle half the rice, then half the rosewater, saffron milk, and lamb. Repeat with the remaining ingredients. Cover the dish with foil and bake for 1 hour in an oven preheated to 300°F.

Serves 4–6

5 oz ghee or clarified butter (see page 23)

2 cinnamon sticks

6 green cardamom pods

6 cloves

1 lb 5 oz boneless leg of lamb, cut into 1-inch cubes

7 oz yogurt, preferably Greek yogurt, whisked

1 teaspoon red chili powder

2 teaspoons Ginger Paste (see page 22)

a pinch of asafoetida

1/2 teaspoon ground cumin

a pinch of ground cloves

1/2 teaspoon ground green cardamom

11 oz basmati rice

salt to taste

7/8 cup milk

2 pinches of saffron

4 teaspoons rosewater

A *kadhai* is a wok, generally an iron one. Food cooked in a *kadhai* has a distinctive roasted, smoky flavor.

Kadhai Chholey

Chickpeas with tomatoes and chili

1 Drain the chickpeas and put them in a pan with 3½ pints water, the bicarbonate of soda and some salt. Boil until tender, then drain off excess liquid and set aside.

2 Heat the ghee or clarified butter in a pan, add the cumin seeds and cook until they start to crackle. Add the onions and sauté until golden brown, then add the garlic paste and cook, stirring, for 30 seconds. Add the chopped tomatoes, tomato purée, chilies, chholey masala and some salt and stir-fry for 2 minutes.

3 Add the boiled chickpeas and 14 tablespoons water and cook until all the water has been absorbed. Stir in the lemon juice and shredded ginger.

Serves 4–6

9 oz chickpeas, soaked in cold water overnight

¼ teaspoon bicarbonate of soda

3 oz ghee or clarified butter (see page 23)

1 teaspoon cumin seeds

14 oz onions, chopped

1 oz Garlic Paste (see page 22)

1 lb 5 oz tomatoes, chopped

1 tablespoon tomato purée

4 green chilies, chopped

1 oz Chholey Masala (see page 25)

salt to taste

2 tablespoons lemon juice

1½ oz fresh ginger, finely shredded

One of the earliest tandoori restaurants in Delhi was Moti Mahal, owned by refugees fleeing to the city when the country was partitioned in 1947.

Tandoor

Delhi was the capital of kings for a thousand years and the silhouette of seven ancient cities line the sky, among them the ruins of the Old Fort, Tughlaqabad, and the Red Fort built by the Moghul Emperor Shahjahan. The last historic city to be built was New Delhi, designed by the British architect Lutyens when the capital of the Raj was shifted to Delhi from Calcutta in 1911. It's ironic that, despite the fact that the British first arrived in India to search for spices, food at the height of the Raj was made as bland and as much like English food as possible. East Indiamen came for pepper that was needed in Europe to preserve meat and mull wine. Salt was always important—the word salary derives from it because in ancient times Roman soldiers were paid partly in salt—but in the hot Indian climate it is vital. Mahatma Gandhi understood this when he led the famous Salt March that helped to end the Raj.

Meanwhile, after a thousand years of Hindu, Muslim, Sikh, and British influence, Delhi became a unique city in its architecture, food, and culture, but one of the most popular foods with all communities proved to be Tandoori cuisine.

The tandoor, an open clay oven, is an ancient Indian invention. Its circumference is designed to spread heat evenly and tandoori bread is believed to have been made in India for over 5,000 years. There are many variations of tandoori bread: *naan* is made with self-rising flour kneaded with yogurt and milk; the flaky, layered *parantha* is wholemeal flour kneaded with oil or ghee; and a tandoori *roti* is a lighter version of the tandoori *parantha*, minus the oil/ghee.

There are three types of tandoors—the small domestic tandoor made of clay and iron; the much larger commercial tandoor with brick walls that are cemented; and the biggest of all, the commercial iron tandoor used to bake rich butter *rotis* and other delicacies. The mouth of the tandoor should be near the cook and the opening at the bottom facing away from him so that he does not feel the heat. Coal or coke is the preferred medium for tandoori cooking to provide a slow, medium heat.

It was only when the use of meat tenderizers, such as papaya, was properly understood that meat began to be cooked in the tandoor. Marination is very important in tandoori cooking and the most widely used tenderizers are kachri pod, raw papaya, and yogurt. All three are often used when cooking *raan mussalam*, for example, since it's a whole leg of lamb and, if well marinated, it melts in the mouth.

Malai means creamy, an apt description of the succulent kebabs in this recipe.

Malai Kebab

Chicken kebabs

1 Mix the chicken with all the ingredients for the first marinade and set aside for 30 minutes.

2 Mix together all the ingredients for the second marinade to form a thick paste and season with salt. Add the chicken pieces, mix well and set aside for 2 hours.

3 Put the chicken pieces on skewers and cook in an oven preheated to 350°F for 15 minutes, or in a moderately hot tandoor oven for 6–8 minutes. Baste with the oil and cook for another 2–3 minutes.

4 Squeeze the lemon juice on to the chicken and sprinkle over the chat masala. Serve with the onion, tomato and lettuce, if liked.

Serves 4–6

2¼ lb boneless chicken
breasts, cut into bite-sized
pieces
7 tablespoons vegetable oil

For the first marinade:

4 tablespoons lemon juice
1 teaspoon Ginger Paste (see page 22)
1 teaspoon Garlic Paste (see page 22)
salt to taste

For the second marinade:

5 oz cream cheese
1¾ cup light cream
a pinch of ground nutmeg
a pinch of ground mace
½ teaspoon ground green cardamom
½ teaspoon ground white pepper
1 teaspoon finely chopped green chili
2 tablespoons finely chopped fresh coriander
1 teaspoon finely chopped fresh ginger

To serve:

½ teaspoon lemon juice
¼ teaspoon Chat Masala (see page 23)
1 onion, very thinly sliced
1 tomato, sliced
2 lettuce leaves, shredded

Sole or pomfret could be substituted for the trout.

A small salad of onion, tomato, and lettuce can be served with the fish.

Tandoori Machhi

Tandoori trout

Serves 4–6

4 9 oz trout, cleaned
¹/₂ cup vegetable oil

**For the first
marinade:**

4 tablespoons lemon juice
1 teaspoon Ginger Paste (see
    page 22)
1 teaspoon Garlic Paste (see
    page 22)
salt to taste

**For the second
marinade:**

4 teaspoons gram flour
    (chickpea flour), fried in
    4 teaspoons ghee until it
    turns a very pale brown
4 tablespoons vegetable oil
1 teaspoon Ginger Paste (see
    page 22)
1 teaspoon Garlic Paste (see
    page 22)
12 oz yogurt, preferably
    Greek yogurt, whisked
salt to taste

8 oz fresh coriander, coarsely
    chopped
4 oz mint, coarsely chopped
4 green chilies, chopped
4 garlic cloves, chopped
1¹/₂-inch piece of fresh ginger,
    chopped
2 teaspoons dried mango
    powder
¹/₂ teaspoon cumin seeds, dry-
    roasted in a frying pan and
    then ground

To serve:

2 tablespoons lemon juice
¹/₂ teaspoon Chat Masala (see
    page 23)

1 Make 3–4 deep cuts on each side of the trout. Mix together all the ingredients for the first marinade, rub over the trout, and set aside for 30 minutes.

2 Put all the ingredients for the second marinade in a blender, add some salt, and process until smooth. Spread the marinade over the trout and set aside for 2 hours.

3 Put the fish on a rack over a baking tray and cook in an oven preheated to 350°F for 20 minutes, or in a moderately hot tandoor for 10–12 minutes. Baste with the vegetable oil and then cook for a further 2–3 minutes.

4 Sprinkle the lemon juice and chat masala over the trout and serve.

Carom seeds, also known as lovage,

take the delicious salmon to new taste horizons.

Salmon Ka Tikka

Marinated salmon

Serves 4–6
2¼ lb salmon fillets, skinned
   and cut into bite-sized
   pieces
7 tablespoons vegetable oil

**For the first
marinade:**
½ cup lemon juice
1 teaspoon Ginger Paste (see
   page 22)
1 teaspoon Garlic Paste (see
   page 22)
salt to taste

**For the second
marinade:**
2 tablespoons chopped fresh
   dill
1¾ cup light cream
1 tablespoon honey
¼ teaspoon carom seeds
1½ teaspoons Dijon mustard
5 oz cream cheese
1 teaspoon ground green
   cardamom
½ teaspoon crushed black
   peppercorns
salt to taste

To serve:
2 tablespoons lemon juice
½ teaspoon Chat Masala (see
   page 23)
1 onion, very thinly sliced
1 tomato, sliced
2 lettuce leaves, shredded

1 Mix together all the ingredients for the first marinade, add
the salmon pieces, and mix well. Set aside for 30 minutes.

2 Mix all the ingredients for the second marinade to a smooth
paste, adding salt to taste, and mix with the fish. Set aside for
2 hours.

3 Put the salmon pieces on skewers and cook in an oven
preheated to 350°F for 10 minutes, or in a moderately hot
tandoor for 4–5 minutes. Baste with the vegetable oil and cook
for a further minute or two.

4 Sprinkle the lemon juice and chat masala over the salmon and
serve with the onion, tomato, and lettuce.

Yogurt is a natural tenderizer and, in dishes like this,

keeps the meat juicy and succulent, ensuring that the cooking time is as brief as possible.

Tandoori Murg

Tandoori chicken

Serves 4–6

1 lb 7 oz whole skinned chicken, jointed into 4 pieces (a chicken this size is ideal for cooking in a tandoor oven but in a conventional oven you could use a bigger bird)

3 tablespoons vegetable oil

For the first marinade:

4 tablespoons lemon juice

1/4 teaspoon red chili powder

1/2 oz Ginger Paste (see page 22)

1 oz Garlic Paste (see page 22)

salt to taste

For the second marinade:

9 oz yogurt, preferably Greek yogurt, whisked

1 teaspoon lemon juice

5 tablespoons vegetable oil

1/4 teaspoon red chili powder

a pinch of Garam Masala (see page 24)

salt to taste

1/2 teaspoon cumin seeds, dry-roasted in a frying pan and then ground

a pinch of ground fenugreek leaves

a pinch of ground green cardamom

To serve:

1/2 teaspoon lemon juice

1/4 teaspoon Chat Masala (see page 23)

1 red onion, very thinly sliced in rings

lemon wedges

1 With a sharp knife, make 3 deep parallel cuts on each chicken breast, 2 parallel cuts on each thigh, and 3 on each leg.

2 Mix together all the ingredients for the first marinade to a paste and rub it all over the chicken. Set aside for 30 minutes.

3 Mix together all the ingredients for the second marinade, adding salt to taste, and use to coat the chicken. Set aside for 2 hours.

4 Put the chicken pieces on a baking sheet and cook in an oven preheated to 350°F for 25–30 minutes, or in a moderately hot tandoor oven for 12–15 minutes. Baste the chicken with the vegetable oil and cook for a further 2–3 minutes.

5 Squeeze the lemon juice on to the chicken and then sprinkle over the chat masala. Serve with the onion rings and lemon wedges.

Variation: Chicken Tikka

This is the same as tandoori chicken but uses boneless meat. Cut the chicken into bite-sized pieces, then marinate it as described, left. Reduce the cooking time to 15 minutes if using a conventional oven and 6–8 minutes if using a tandoor.

The *raan* can be served with gravy made with the leftover juices in the pan. Just add water, stir and cook for a few minutes.

Raan Mussalam

Roast lamb

Serves 4–6

1 leg of spring lamb, weighing about 1 3/4 lb (5 lb with bone)

For the first marinade:

2 tablespoons malt vinegar
1 tablespoon red chili powder
1 tablespoon Ginger Paste (see page 22)
1 1/2 tablespoons Garlic Paste (see page 22)
5 tablespoons vegetable oil
salt to taste

For the second marinade:

7 oz yogurt, preferably Greek yogurt, whisked
1/2 teaspoon ground cumin
1/2 teaspoon ground coriander
1/2 teaspoon Garam Masala (see page 24)
1 tablespoon paprika
1/4 teaspoon ground black cardamom
1/4 teaspoon ground green cardamom
a pinch of ground nutmeg
a pinch of ground cloves
1 bay leaf
1 teaspoon rosewater
1/4 teaspoon ground cinnamon
salt to taste

To serve:

2 tablespoons lemon juice
1/2 teaspoon Chat Masala (see page 23)
1 scallion, cut lengthways into thin shreds

1 Prick the leg of lamb all over with a fork. Mix together all the ingredients for the first marinade, spread over the meat, and set aside for 2 hours.

2 Mix all the ingredients for the second marinade to a smooth paste, season with salt, and spread the mixture all over the lamb. Put it in a roasting pan, cover with foil, and cook in an oven preheated to 300°F for 3 hours.

3 Remove the meat from the oven, take it off the bone, and cut it into bite-sized pieces. Pour the lemon juice on it, sprinkle with the chat masala and mix well. Arrange on a serving platter and decorate with the spring onion shreds.

Although the meat is taken off the bone after roasting,
traditionally the lamb bone is served on the plate.

Subz Kebab can be made from any combination of vegetables—except root vegetables such as potatoes, which can be skewered pre-cooked and then marinated.

Subz Kebab

Vegetable shashlik

1 Mix together all the ingredients for the marinade. Pour the marinade over the vegetables and paneer, if using, and set aside for 30 minutes. Soak some wooden skewers in cold water for 30 minutes.

2 Put the vegetables, and paneer if using, on the skewers and cook in an oven preheated to 350°F for 20 minutes or in a moderately hot tandoor for 10 minutes. Baste with the vegetable oil and cook for a further 2–3 minutes.

3 Sprinkle the vegetables with the lemon juice and chat masala.

Serves 4–6

7 oz red peppers, cut into
  1-inch squares
7 oz green peppers, cut into
  1-inch squares
7 oz yellow peppers, cut into
  1-inch squares
7 oz button mushrooms,
  left whole
7 oz baby eggplants, cut
  in half
7 oz tomatoes, cut into
  1-inch cubes
7 oz onions, cut into
  1-inch squares
7 oz zucchini, cut into
  1-inch cubes
7 oz paneer, cut into 1-inch
  cubes (optional)
2 tablespoons vegetable oil

For the marinade:
8 tablespoons yogurt,
  preferably Greek yogurt,
  whisked
1 teaspoon Ginger Paste (see
  page 22)
2 teaspoons Garlic Paste (see
  page 22)
4 teaspoons lemon juice
3 tablespoons vegetable oil

1 teaspoon Garam Masala
  (see page 24)
1 teaspoon ground
  pomegranate seeds
1 teaspoon crushed black
  peppercorns
1 teaspoon ground green
  cardamom
1 teaspoon ground anise seeds
1 teaspoon dry mango powder
2 teaspoons ground coriander
1 teaspoon ground cumin
1 teaspoon red chili powder
1 1/2 teaspoons Chat Masala
  (see page 23)
salt to taste

To serve:
2 tablespoons lemon juice
1/2 teaspoon Chat Masala (see
  page 23)

Traditional Indians, including Bengalis, eat with their fingers
and always with the right hand which is considered pure,
unlike the left hand that is used for ablutions.

Bengal

In Bengal, they consider fish to be a vegetarian dish, jokingly referred to either as *jal tori* (water gourd) or as the Fruit of the Ocean. Even Bengali Brahmins eat fish, although Brahmins are normally vegetarian. With numerous ponds, rivers and the teeming waters of the Bay of Bengal, it is no wonder that the people are enthusiastic "fishetarians." However, a wide variety of vegetables also grow in the hot and humid climate, including the popular bananas that are eaten ripe, raw and cooked.

Bengal was linked to the rest of the world by trade from ancient times, especially with Armenia, Persia, Greece, and China. Almost a hundred years before the British arrived, the Portuguese built a church and a township there. In 1690, Joe Charnock of the East India Company arrived at the mouth of the River Hooghly, at Kalighat, a place named after its presiding deity, the Goddess Kali. Later, East Indiamen created Calcutta (now called Kolkatta) and it became the capital of the British Raj. It is said that the first meal Charnock was offered by local villagers was *khitchuri*, a dish of rice and lentils. That evolved into kedgeree, a favored dish of the Raj.

A typical Bengali meal would start with a bitter dish made with bitter gourd, neem leaves, and green bananas, cooked in spices, followed by rice, daal, and fish dishes. The most popular is the river fish Hilsa, a type of herring, typically fried in hot mustard oil with mustard and poppy seeds—mustard is to Bengal what coconut is to Goa, and mustard oil is used for frying while mustard seeds are used in cooking. Fish eyes and heads are considered to be delicacies, but, by convention, fish is not eaten at certain times of year that coincide with their breeding cycles.

The plentiful rice of Bengal is not the basmati of North India. Instead, there are other varieties such as Gopal and Kamini. A lot of Bengali rice is parboiled—a healthy method because the grain retains the vitamins and nutrients contained in the husk. Cooking perfect rice was the test of a good cook in Bengal and a new daughter-in-law could curry favor with her in-laws if she could do that successfully.

The other distinct taste of Bengal is a sweet one. Milk-based sweets such as *rasmalai, rabri, rosogolla, sondesh,* and *chenna* are now popular all over India. In Bengali homes the meal could end with *mishti doi,* curd sweetened with dates, and a plate of dry sweets. Finally, a *paan,* betel-leaf, would put a full-stop to the meal, acting both as a digestive and mouth freshener.

Traditionally, the smallest shrimp with their shells on, for a crunchy effect, would be used in this dish. Here we have peeled them.

Jheenga Charchari

Stir-fried shrimp

1 Grind together the cumin, poppy, and mustard seeds, turmeric, red chilies, onion, ginger, and garlic.

2 In a large frying pan, heat the mustard oil to smoking point. Add all the tempering spices and let them splutter until the dried chilies change color.

3 Add the ground spice mixture and stir-fry for 1 minute. Then add the shrimp and stir-fry over a high heat for 2 minutes. Stir in the sugar and some salt and cook for about a minute longer, until the oil separates from the mixture.

Serves 4–6

1 teaspoon cumin seeds
1 teaspoon poppy seeds
1 teaspoon mustard seeds
1 teaspoon ground turmeric
4 dried red chilies
1 large onion, chopped
1 ¹/₂-inch piece of fresh ginger, chopped
5 garlic cloves, chopped
2¹/₄ lb medium-sized raw headless shrimp, shelled and deveined
1 teaspoon sugar
salt to taste

For tempering:
3 tablespoons mustard oil
2 dried red chilies
2 bay leaves
1¹/₂ teaspoons whole Panch Phoran Spice Mix (see page 24)

A traditional Muslim dish, these kebabs are simmered

in a *masala* (mixture) of spices and condiments.

Husseini Murg Masala

Husseini chicken curry

1 Arrange the chicken pieces, peppers, and onions alternately on ten 6 inch skewers and set aside.

2 Heat the ghee or clarified butter in a pan, add the whole spices, and let them splutter for 20 seconds. Add the onions and fry until brown.

3 Add the chilli powder, turmeric, yogurt, ginger, and garlic pastes and stir-fry until the oil separates from the mixture. Then add the sugar and some salt to taste. Bring to a boil and cook for 5 minutes.

4 Carefully add the skewers to the mixture and cook for 10–15 minutes, until the meat is tender and the sauce has a coating consistency. Serve in the sauce, or remove the skewers and serve the sauce separately.

Serves 4–6

2¼ lb boneless chicken breasts, cut into bite-sized pieces

11 oz green peppers, cut into bite-sized pieces

11 oz red onion, cut into bite-sized pieces

4½ oz ghee or clarified butter (see page 23)

½ teaspoon cloves

1 teaspoon green cardamom pods

2 cinnamon sticks

2 bay leaves

9 oz onions, finely chopped

1 tablespoon red chili powder

1 teaspoon ground turmeric

7 oz yogurt, preferably Greek yogurt, whisked

1 tablespoon Ginger Paste (see page 22)

1 tablespoon Garlic Paste (see page 22)

1 tablespoon sugar

salt to taste

Every Bengali's home-made favorite, this is a simple and superb way to cook fish.

Macher Jhol

Fish curry

1 Mix together half the turmeric, the ginger and garlic pastes and some salt and then mix with the fish. Set aside for 20 minutes.

2 Heat the mustard oil in a pan, add the onion seeds, and fry until they start to splutter. Then add the onions and fry for about 5 minutes, until they just start to turn brown. Add the fish and green chili and fry for 2 minutes.

3 Mix the red chili powder, remaining turmeric and some salt with 7 tablespoons water and add to the pan. Reduce the heat and simmer for 10 minutes, until the sauce thickens slightly, then stir in the lemon juice. Serve with steamed or boiled rice.

Serves 4–6

1 1/2 teaspoons ground
  turmeric
1 teaspoon Ginger Paste (see
  page 22)
1 teaspoon Garlic Paste (see
  page 22)
salt to taste
2 1/4 lb cod or lemon sole
  fillets, skinned and cut into
  bite-sized pieces

7 tablespoons mustard oil
1/4 teaspoon onion seeds
  (nigella seeds)
5 oz onions, thinly sliced
1 teaspoon finely chopped
  green chili
1 teaspoon red chili powder
1 teaspoon lemon juice

Bengal was once the hub of maritime commerce,

and this dish is well known in Malaysia, Singapore, and Thailand.

Chingri Malai Curry

Creamy shrimp curry

Serves 4–6

1 coconut, freshly grated
1 lb 5 oz medium-sized raw
   headless shrimp, shelled
   and deveined
$^1/_4$ teaspoon ground turmeric
salt to taste
2 tablespoons mustard oil
1-inch piece of cinnamon stick

1 blade of mace
1 bay leaf
1 green chili, seeded and finely
   chopped
$^1/_2$ teaspoon ground green
   cardamom
3 cloves, ground

1 Put the grated coconut in a piece of cheesecloth and squeeze it over a bowl to extract the cream. Set the coconut cream aside. Then pour $1^1/_2$ cups of boiling water over the grated coconut, let it stand for 2 minutes, and then squeeze in a piece of cheesecloth again to extract the milk. Keep the cream and milk in different containers.

2 Mix the shrimp with the turmeric and some salt and set aside for 10 minutes. Heat the mustard oil in a large pan, add the shrimp and stir-fry over a high heat until they turn pink. Remove from the pan with a slotted spoon.

3 Add the cinnamon, mace, and bay leaf to the oil and let them splutter for 10 seconds. Stir in the coconut milk and bring to a boil.

4 Add the shrimp, chili, ground cardamom, cloves, and some salt. Cook for 2 minutes, then stir in the coconut cream. This dish goes best with plain boiled rice.

People from as far away as Greece, Mesopotamia, and Persia used to travel to Bengal

to trade and this is just one of the fusion dishes that evolved from the interaction.

Keema Torkaari

Lamb-stuffed vegetables

1 Heat the oil in a pan until it simmers, add the cinnamon sticks and let them splutter for 15 seconds. Add the ground lamb and cook, stirring, until all the juices from the meat dry up.

2 Add the ground spices, onions, green chili, sugar, and some salt and cook, stirring, for 8–10 minutes. Pour in 3½ cups water and simmer until it has all been absorbed and the mixture is dry. Remove from the heat and leave to cool.

3 Prepare all the vegetables by slicing off a lid and making a cavity in each one (don't cut them in half), removing the pulp/seeds/flesh.

4 Fill the vegetables with the meat mixture and bake for 35–45 minutes in an oven preheated to 250°F.

Serves 4–6
7 tablespoons mustard oil
2 cinnamon sticks
2¼ lb ground lamb
¼ teaspoon ground cloves
1 teaspoon ground green
   cardamom
½ teaspoon red chili powder
1 teaspoon ground turmeric
9 oz onions, chopped
1 tablespoon finely chopped
   green chili
2 teaspoons granulated sugar
salt to taste
2 tomatoes

2 baby eggplants
2 green peppers
2 bitter gourds
2 snake gourds

The custom of preparing *Khitchuri* dates back to Aryan times, and many travellers to India have mentioned it in their travelogues. This method is truly time-tested!

K h i t c h u r i

Kedgeree

Serves 4–6

4 oz rice
4 oz split green lentils
1 tablespoon mustard oil
½ teaspoon mustard seeds
½ teaspoon anise seeds
2 green chilies, chopped
1 teaspoon finely chopped
  fresh ginger
¼ teaspoon ground turmeric
salt to taste
fried dried red chilies as
  garnish, optional

1 Soak the rice and lentils in cold water for 30 minutes and then drain.

2 Heat the mustard oil in a pan, add the mustard seeds and anise seeds and let them splutter for 15 seconds. Then add the green chilies, ginger, and turmeric and sauté for 30 seconds.

3 Pour in 1¾ cup water and bring to a boil. Add the soaked rice and lentils and boil for 10 minutes.

4 Reduce the heat to very low, cover the pan, and simmer for 15 minutes, until the rice and lentils are slightly overcooked and mushy. Season to taste with salt. Garnish with the chilies, if using.

Shobjee Jhalfarezi

Fried vegetables

1 Heat the mustard oil in a large pan until it simmers and add the whole spices. Let them splutter for 10 seconds, then add the potatoes and stir-fry for 2–3 minutes.

2 Add all the other vegetables and stir-fry for 3–4 minutes. Stir in the sugar and some salt, cover and cook on a very low heat for 10 minutes, until the vegetables are tender. Mix in the grated coconut, garnish with the coconut shavings, and serve.

Serves 4-6

7 tablespoons mustard oil
½ teaspoon Panch Phoran
  Spice Mix (see page 24)
2 bay leaves
4 oz potatoes, cut into fingers
4 oz wax gourd, cut into
  fingers
4 oz eggplant, cut into fingers
4 oz pumpkin, cut into fingers
1 large onion, cut into thick
  slices horizontally
1 large tomato, cut into thick
  slices horizontally
2 teaspoons sugar
salt to taste
5 tablespoons freshly grated
  coconut
toasted coconut shavings
  to serve

ERECTED TO COMMEMORATE THE LANDING
IN INDIA OF THEIR IMPERIAL MAJESTIES
KING GEORGE V AND QUEEN MARY

"Alphonso" is the king of Bombay mangoes—North India
has different varieties—and the best alphonsos come from
Ratnagiri, where a Mr. Alphonso created the hybrid variety.

Mumbai

Bombay, now renamed Mumbai, on the Arabian Coast smells of the sea and of money. It is the commercial heart of India, home to the country's leading industrialists, to the matinee idols of Bollywood (the giant Hindi film industry), to murderous underworld dons as well as to a large homeless population. It teems with children of different gods—Hindu, Muslim, Sikh, Christian, Jew, Parsee. In the typical multi-layered identity of all Indians, these people are also Maratha, Gujarati, Parsee, Marwari, Anglo-Indian, Punjabi, Tamil, Malyali, and Bihari. Bombay food is as diverse as its population and as complex as its history.

The original people to inhabit the group of seven islands that is modern Mumbai were the Koli fishermen. Then the rulers of Gujarat annexed the islands. In 1534 the Portuguese forced the Shah of Gujarat to transfer the islands to them and they called them Bom Baim—Good Harbor. In 1661, the English King Charles II married Catherine, sister of the Portuguese king, and she brought him Bombay in her dowry.

The gifts of the hot, tropical Arabian coast are the coconut, a huge variety of seafood, and a good climate for growing fruit and vegetables, but each community developed its own distinctive cuisine. If the scholarly Brahmins are vegetarian, the warrior Marathas eat anything and one of their typical dishes is quails marinated in yogurt and spices, wrapped in wet clay, and baked in an open fire.

The Koli fishing community eat very spicy food, cooked with coconut and green chilies, and use a special, pepperlike spice called *chircoot* for cooking fish. Fish such as newta, pomfret, surmai, shrimp and crab are widely eaten. Even the Bombay duck is not duck at all but is dried fish.

Irani/Parsee restaurants popularized dishes such as *keema pao* (curried mince served with bread), *akuri* (made with eggs), and *patra* fish (baked in a banana leaf packet). The Bohri Muslim community developed their own distinctive style of cooking with dishes such as *palida* (thick broth) and *dabba-ghosht* (meat loaf). Mumbai's big Gujarati community is largely vegetarian, and they add a touch of sugar to most of their dishes.

Mumbai's street foods such as *bhel-poori* (a spicy dish of puffed rice, tamarind chutney, onions, green chilies), *pohe* (dry dish of pressed rice, onions and chilies), and *bhajjias* (made of onions or potatoes) are now eaten all over the country.

Fried fish is eaten more as a street snack in Bombay, and is especially popular all along the coast. Each seller selfishly guards the family recipe for the marinade mix.

Fried fish with aromatic spices; no dip is necessary as all the intended flavors are coated on the fish itself.

Tali Machi Masala

Fried fish

1 Mix together the turmeric, chili powder, lemon juice, ginger and garlic pastes and some salt. Spread this mixture over the fish fillets and set aside for 30 minutes.

2 Dust the fish in the flour, then in the rice flour and deep-fry in the vegetable oil for about 2 minutes, until crisp. Drain on paper toweling and serve with a lemon wedge.

Serves 4–6

$^1/_2$ teaspoon ground turmeric
1 teaspoon red chili powder
$^1/_2$ teaspoon lemon juice
$^1/_2$ teaspoon Ginger Paste (see page 22)
$^1/_2$ teaspoon Garlic Paste (see page 22)
salt to taste
$2^1/_4$ lb pomfret fillets (or other white fish fillets), skinned
4 oz all-purpose flour
4 oz rice flour
$3^1/_2$ cups vegetable oil
lemon wedges to serve

The Parsee community in Bombay, originally from Persia, have cooked this family favorite for generations, and it is now enjoyed by all.

Murg Farcha

Fried chicken

Serves 4–6

1 chicken, skinned and cut
  into 8 pieces
1 tablespoon malt vinegar
$^1/_2$ teaspoon red chili powder
a pinch of ground turmeric
salt to taste
Tamatar ki Chutney (Tomato
  chutney), to serve (see page
  133)

For frying:

4 eggs, lightly beaten
$^1/_2$ teaspoon Curry Powder
  (see page 23)
a pinch of red chili powder
a pinch of ground turmeric
1 teaspoon finely chopped
  fresh mint
1 tablespoon finely chopped
  fresh coriander
$^1/_2$ teaspoon finely chopped
  green chili
7 oz dried breadcrumbs
1 quart vegetable oil

1 Mix the chicken pieces with the malt vinegar, chili powder, turmeric, and some salt and set aside for 1 hour. Place in a steamer and steam for 15 minutes, then leave to cool.

2 Mix together all the ingredients for frying except the breadcrumbs and oil. Coat the chicken pieces in this mixture and then roll them in the breadcrumbs. Repeat once more.

3 Deep-fry the chicken pieces in the hot oil until crisp and cooked through, then drain on paper toweling and serve with some Tomato chutney.

This recipe is ideal for rejuvenating leftovers. Any vegetables or meat can be treated in the same way. Serve with naan bread.

K e e m a   P a r   A n d a

Spicy minced lamb with egg

1 Heat 7 tablespoons of the oil in a large pan, add the cumin seeds and dried chilies, and fry for 5 seconds. Add the onions and fry until golden brown.

2 Add the ginger, garlic, chili powder, turmeric, tomatoes, and some salt and cook, stirring, for about 10 minutes, until the oil separates from the mixture.

3 Add the ground lamb and cook for about 25 minutes, until all the juices from the meat have dried up and the oil has separated out again.

4 Heat the remaining 1 tablespoon oil in a frying pan and fry the eggs. Serve the meat garnished with the fried eggs.

Serves 4–6

$^1/_2$ cup vegetable oil
$^1/_2$ teaspoon cumin seeds
6 small dried red chilies
5 oz onions, chopped
1 teaspoon finely chopped
   fresh ginger
1 teaspoon finely chopped
   garlic
$^1/_2$ teaspoon red chili powder
$^1/_3$ teaspoon ground turmeric
4 oz tomatoes, chopped
salt to taste
$2^1/_4$ lb ground lamb
4 eggs

The Parsee community in Bombay love food and each
meal consists of endless courses, each a delight to savor.

A traditional Parsee recipe. The matchstick potatoes

can be bought ready to fry from Indian shops.

Salli Gosht

Lamb with straw potatoes

Serves 4–6

3 tablespoons vegetable oil
3 bay leaves
3 cloves
2 cinnamon sticks
½ teaspoon cumin seeds
4 tablespoons chopped onion
2¼ lb boneless leg of lamb, cut into bite-sized pieces
1 tablespoon Ginger Paste (see page 22)
1 teaspoon Garlic Paste (see page 22)

5 fresh curry leaves
2 teaspoons red chili powder
1 teaspoon ground coriander
salt to taste
7 oz tomatoes, chopped
2 tablespoons crushed palm sugar
½ teaspoon Garam Masala (see page 24)
2 medium potatoes, peeled, cut into matchsticks, and deep-fried until golden
1 tablespoon chopped fresh coriander (optional)

1 Heat the oil in a large pan and add the whole spices. Then add the onion and fry until golden brown.

2 Add the lamb, ginger and garlic pastes, curry leaves, chili powder, ground coriander, and some salt and cook, stirring, for about 20 minutes, until the juices from the meat dry up.

3 Add the tomatoes and cook, stirring, for 10 minutes, then add 3½ cups water and the palm sugar. Bring to a boil and cook for 25 minutes, or until the meat is tender and the sauce has thickened.

4 Stir in the garam masala, then sprinkle the matchstick potatoes, and chopped fresh coriander if using, on top and serve.

Saar denotes a wet vegetable dish. It is ideal to eat

with rice or *pooris* (see page 131).

Tamatar, Phool Gobi, Gajjar Che Saar

Mixed vegetable curry

1 Heat the oil in a large pan, add the mustard seeds and cumin seeds, and let them crackle for 5 seconds. Then add the ginger, garlic, green chili, curry leaves, and chili powder and sauté for 15 seconds.

2 Add the vegetables, sugar, and some salt and stir-fry for 1 minute. Stir in the puréed tomatoes, bring to a boil, and cook until the vegetables are tender.

3 Stir in the coconut, fresh coriander and ground black pepper and serve.

Serves 4–6

4 *tablespoons vegetable oil*
¹/₂ teaspoon mustard seeds
¹/₂ teaspoon cumin seeds
1 *teaspoon finely chopped fresh ginger*
1 *teaspoon finely chopped garlic*
1 *green chili, finely chopped*
6 *fresh curry leaves*
¹/₄ teaspoon red chili powder
11 *oz prepared vegetables, such as sugar snap peas, carrots, green beans, cauliflower, zucchini, etc.*
a pinch of sugar
salt to taste
11 *oz fresh tomatoes, puréed*
2 *tablespoons grated coconut*
1 *tablespoon chopped fresh coriander*
¹/₄ teaspoon ground black pepper

The curried eggplant rice goes very well with the *Bhindi ki Kadhi*.

Vanghi Bhaat

Rice with eggplant

1 Heat the oil in a large pan, add the cloves, mustard seeds, and cinnamon sticks and cook for 10 seconds, until they start to crackle.

2 Add the eggplant, cashew nuts, asafoetida, ground turmeric, and green chilies, and stir-fry for 2 minutes.

3 Add all the other ground spices, plus the yogurt, rice, some salt and 2½ cups water. Bring to a boil, stir the rice once, and cook over a medium heat for 6–8 minutes, until the rice has absorbed all the water.

4 Reduce the heat to its lowest, cover the pan with a lid, and cook for 20 minutes. Add the grated coconut and chopped fresh coriander, mix well and serve.

Serves 4–6

3 tablespoons vegetable oil
4 cloves
½ teaspoon mustard seeds
2 cinnamon sticks
7 oz eggplant, cut into ½-inch dice
12–15 cashew nuts
a pinch of asafoetida
½ teaspoon ground turmeric
2 green chilies, cut in half
½ teaspoon ground coriander
½ teaspoon ground cumin
⅓ teaspoon red chili powder
salt to taste
2 tablespoons yogurt, preferably Greek yogurt, whisked
1 lb 2 oz basmati rice
1 coconut, freshly grated
4 oz fresh coriander, chopped

Bhindi Ki Kadhi

Fried okra in sauce

1 Whisk together the yogurt, gram flour and some salt and set aside. Heat 3¾ cups oil for deep-frying, add the okra, and deep-fry over a medium heat until crisp. Remove and drain on paper toweling.

2 Heat the 5 tablespoons vegetable oil in a pan, add the cumin seeds, onion seeds, dried chilies, and asafoetida and fry for 10 seconds, until they begin to splutter. Add the onions and fry for about 10 minutes, until golden brown. Add the garlic paste and cook, stirring, for 1 minute.

3 Add the chili powder and turmeric and cook, stirring, for 30 seconds. Then add the yogurt mixture and bring to a boil. Reduce the heat and simmer for 20 minutes. Stir in the chopped fresh coriander and fried okra and serve.

Serves 4–6

1 lb 2 oz yogurt, preferably Greek yogurt, whisked
6 tablespoons gram flour (chickpea flour)
salt to taste
3¾ cups plus 5 tablespoons vegetable oil
2¼ lb okra
½ teaspoon cumin seeds
a pinch of onion seeds (nigella seeds)
4 dried red chilies
a pinch of asafoetida
2 onions, chopped
1½ teaspoons Garlic Paste (see page 22)
½ teaspoon red chili powder
½ teaspoon ground turmeric
4 tablespoons chopped fresh coriander

Grated raw mangoes transform the *chitranna* into something truly memorable.

Coconut rice, or *bhaat*, is made thoughout southern India, from Bombay to Cochin.

Chitranna

Mango rice

1 Heat 1 tablespoon of the oil in a pan, add the rice and stir-fry for 1 minute. Add 1½ cups plus 1 tablespoon water and bring to a boil. Cook for about 10 minutes, until the rice has absorbed most of the water, then stir the rice carefully so as not to break the grains. Reduce the heat to very low, cover the pan, and cook for about 20 minutes longer, until the rice is tender. Set aside.

2 Heat the remaining oil in a wok. Add the mustard seeds, red chilies, asafoetida, and turmeric and fry for 5 seconds. Add the black gram beans, roasted *channa dal* and peanuts and stir for 10 seconds.

3 Add the cooked rice, grated mango, sugar, and some salt and mix well. Stir in the lemon juice.

Serves 4–6

3 tablespoons vegetable oil
9 oz basmati rice
1 teaspoon mustard seeds
5 dried red chilies
a pinch of asafoetida
a pinch of ground turmeric
2 teaspoons urad dal *(black gram beans)*
4½ oz roasted channa dal *(yellow split peas)*
3 tablespoons peanuts
2 tablespoons grated green unripe mango
½ teaspoon sugar
salt to taste
2 teaspoons lemon juice

Nariyal Bhaat

Coconut rice

1 Heat the oil in a casserole, add the mustard seeds, and let them splutter for 5 seconds. Add the green chili, ginger, and curry leaves and fry for 15 seconds.

2 Add the rice and fry for 1 minute. Add the coconut milk and some salt and bring to a boil. Simmer until most of the coconut milk has been absorbed.

3 Cover the casserole with foil, transfer to an oven preheated to 400°F and bake for 20 minutes. Add the grated coconut and chopped fresh coriander and mix well.

Serves 4–6

4 tablespoons vegetable oil
¼ teaspoon mustard seeds
¼ teaspoon finely chopped green chili
½ teaspoon finely chopped fresh ginger
6 fresh curry leaves
9 oz basmati rice
1½ cups plus 1 tablespoon coconut milk
salt to taste
5 oz grated coconut
1 tablespoon chopped fresh coriander

Serve these tasty eggplant on a bed of turmeric rice—cook basmati rice in water to which turmeric powder has been added. This gives the rice a delicate yellow color.

Vanghi

Spiced baby eggplant

1 Dry-roast the coconut and sesame seeds in a frying pan until golden brown. Set aside.

2 Heat 1 tablespoon oil in a pan, add the onion, and fry until golden brown. Add all the spices, plus the roasted coconut and sesame seeds, the garlic, tamarind paste, jaggery, mango powder, and some salt. Remove from the heat and grind to a smooth paste.

3 Slice the eggplants lengthways into quarters, leaving them attached at the stem. Apply some of the paste along the cut sides of the eggplant.

4 Heat the remaining oil in a large pan over a low heat and add the eggplant. Spread the remaining paste on top of them and cook for 8–10 minutes, until tender, adding a little water if necessary to make a sauce. Serve topped with the shreds of chili.

Serves 4–6

6 tablespoons grated coconut
½ teaspoon sesame seeds
2 tablespoons vegetable oil
4 tablespoons chopped onion
1 teaspoon Goda Masala (see page 25)
½ teaspoon red chili powder
½ teaspoon Garam Masala (see page 24)
2 garlic cloves, crushed
2 teaspoons tamarind paste
1 teaspoon crushed jaggery
½ teaspoon dried mango powder
salt to taste
9 oz baby eggplant
2 green chilies, deseeded and cut into fine julienne shreds

ORA
PRO NOBIS

Goa's distinctive alcoholic *feni*, made from cashew nut and coconut, is said to have been distilled originally by monks.

Goa

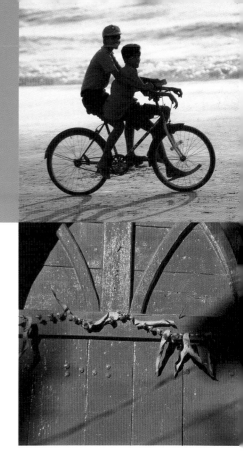

Goa is referred to as Gove—paradise—in the *Puranas*, the ancient books of Indian wisdom. It is still a paradise, with long beaches, palm trees waving in the sea breeze, and children selling fresh fruit on the beach, like useful cherubs. Tiny restaurants in beach shacks offer to cook fresh fish from the morning's catch. The juice of fresh *daab*, green coconut, completes the meal but on breezy moonlit nights the strong *feni*, coconut alcohol, can make the stars look much bigger and brighter.

Because of being on the Konkan coast, the main ingredients of cooking here are rice, fish, coconut and chilies. Fishermen set out to sea at dawn and return loaded with fresh fish—mackerel, pomfret, and dozens of other varieties—that is sold then and there on the beach; a number of the fish sellers are women. The fish that remains unsold is dried in the hot sun.

Goan fish curries are legendary. Marinated in ground chili paste, turmeric, and vinegar, the fish could be fried, or stuffed and then fried. Shrimp *balchao*, for example, is made with vinegar and chopped onions. The abundant coconut is used in full: its milk is used in cooking, its flesh is good for garnishes, and coconut oil is the main cooking medium.

Goa was ruled by Hindus and then Muslims, followed by the Catholic Portuguese, so it became a land of Catholic churches, Hindu temples, Portuguese forts, and mosques. A succession of Hindu dynasties ruled until 1472 A.D., when the Muslim Sultan of Bijapur took over. In 1510 A.D. the Portuguese commander Alfonso de Albuquerque conquered Goa. Albuquerque built a number of impressive buildings in old Goa, the most famous of which is the Basilica of Bom Jesus that houses the 360-year-old mummy of St. Francis Xavier.

Goan cuisine reflects this intense mix of religions and cultures. The Mediterranean influence of the Portuguese is obvious in festive dishes such as roast suckling pig, also found in other Latin cultures. Pork is eaten in many forms, including sausages. *Sorpotel* is a fiery Goanese dish, traditionally made with pork cooked in vinegar. *Vindaloo* is another favourite dish, with more gravy than *sorpotel* and a little more sour. Garlic is used liberally, especially for *vindaloo* and *sorpotel*, when it is mixed with chilies and vinegar. Goan vinegar is made from toddy, which is distilled from the sap of palm trees.

Large raw shrimp can be substituted for the lobster if preferred. Remove the head and shell of each one and the dark intestinal vein running down the tail. Proceed as in step 4 below.

Jheenga Masala

Lobster in the shell

1 Kill the lobsters by plunging them into a very large pan of boiling salted water and boiling for 2 minutes. Drain well, then cut them lengthways in half, remove and discard the stomach sac from just behind the eyes and take out the dark intestinal vein running down the tail. Take out all the meat and reserve, discarding the gills. Cut the meat into large cubes.

2 Heat the oil in a pan, add the carom seeds, and let them crackle for 5 seconds. Add the ginger and garlic and fry until soft. Then add the onions and fry until they are limp but not colored.

3 Dissolve the powdered rice in ½ cup water. Add to the pan with the coconut cream, sugar, turmeric, and some salt and bring to a boil. Cook for 2 minutes.

4 Add the lobster and green chilies and cook for about 5 minutes, until the lobster is tender. Serve the lobster masala in the lobster shells with a boiled rice accompaniment.

Serves 4–6

2 large live lobsters
7 tablespoons vegetable oil
¼ teaspoon carom seeds
3 tablespoons finely shredded fresh ginger
10 garlic cloves, sliced
2 onions, sliced
2 tablespoons raw rice, ground to a powder
2 cups plus 2 tablespoons coconut cream
1 tablespoon sugar
½ teaspoon ground turmeric
salt to taste
5 green chilies, cut into fine shreds

This dish is one of the regulars eaten daily by Goanese. Many dishes in Goa have only

English or Portuguese names, reflecting their Portuguese legacy.

Goan Shrimp Curry

1 Heat the oil in a pan, add the onions, and cook, stirring, for 3 minutes, or until softened. Add the ginger and green chilies and cook for 1 minute.

2 Add the turmeric, coriander, chili powder, and cumin and mix well over a moderate heat. Dissolve the creamed coconut in 1 cup water. Stir it into the pan and cook until the oil separates from the mixture.

3 Add the tamarind and coconut milk, bring to a boil, reduce the heat to low, and simmer for 15 minutes.

4 Wash the shrimp in cold water and drain thoroughly in a colander or sieve. Drop the shrimp into the sauce, add some salt, and simmer gently for about 5 minutes, until the shrimp are cooked. The sauce should have a pouring consistency. Garnish with the coconut slivers, if using, and serve with steamed rice.

Serves 4–6

3 tablespoons vegetable oil
9 oz onions, thinly sliced
2 tablespoons chopped fresh ginger
2 green chilies, finely chopped
a pinch of ground turmeric
1 teaspoon ground coriander
1 teaspoon red chili powder
1 teaspoon ground cumin
2 oz coconut cream
1 tablespoon tamarind paste
½ cup coconut milk
1¾ lb medium-sized raw headless shrimp, shelled and deveined
salt to taste
slivers of coconut to garnish (optional)

A typical Goan dish, this is also made with pork. *Vindaloo* is a Portuguese term for a dish made with vinegar and chilies.

Chicken Vindaloo

1 Mix together all the ground spices with some salt and rub them on to the chicken pieces. Set aside for 1 hour.

2 Heat the oil in a pan and add the garlic paste. Stir-fry for 2 minutes, then add the onion paste. Stir-fry for 5 minutes, then add the ginger paste. Stir-fry for 2 minutes.

3 Add the chicken pieces and cook for 10 minutes. Stir in all the remaining ingredients and $^1/_3$ cup water and simmer for 10 minutes. The sauce should have reduced to a coating consistency. Serve with boiled rice.

Serves 4–6

a pinch of ground turmeric
$^1/_2$ teaspoon red chili powder
1 teaspoon ground coriander
$^1/_4$ teaspoon ground cinnamon
$^1/_4$ teaspoon ground cloves
1 teaspoon ground cumin
$^1/_2$ teaspoon ground black pepper
salt to taste
1 lb 5 oz boneless chicken, cut into bite-sized pieces
3 tablespoons vegetable oil
1 teaspoon Garlic Paste (see page 22)
11 oz Raw Onion Paste (see page 22)
1 teaspoon Ginger Paste (see page 22)
9 oz potatoes, peeled and cut into 1-inch cubes
$1^1/_2$ teaspoons sugar
3 tablespoons malt vinegar
3 tablespoons tomato paste

Bay leaves, cinnamon, and cloves grow in abundance in Goa,

and were discovered by the Portuguese settlers, who created this hearty dish.

Lamb Assadu

Lamb with cinnamon and cloves

Serves 4–6

3/4 cup vegetable oil

2 bay leaves

3 cloves

1-inch piece of cinnamon stick

1 teaspoon Garlic Paste (see
 page 22)

3 dried red chilies

11 oz onions, thickly sliced

2¼ lb boneless leg of lamb, cut
 into 1-inch cubes

½ teaspoon ground turmeric

1 teaspoon paprika

salt to taste

2 tablespoons malt vinegar

4 tomatoes, sliced

fresh bay leaves (optional)

1 Heat the oil in a large pan, add the bay leaves, cloves, and cinnamon stick and let them splutter for a few seconds. Then add the garlic paste and dried red chilies and sauté for 10 seconds.

2 Add the onions and cook, stirring, for about 10 minutes, until golden brown. Add the lamb, turmeric, paprika, and some salt and cook, stirring, for 15 minutes.

3 Pour in 2 cups plus 2 tablespoons water and bring to a boil, then cover and cook for 25 minutes.

4 Stir in the vinegar and cook until the sauce has reduced to a coating consistency. Arrange the tomato slices, and bay leaves if using, on top and serve with boiled rice.

Start the preparation the night before or on the morning you are cooking, to allow time for the marination of the chicken.

Chicken Cafrael

Serves 4–6

2¼ lb boneless chicken thighs, cut into bite-sized pieces
3½ cups vegetable oil
fresh mint leaves to garnish

For the marinade:

1 teaspoon Ginger Paste (see page 22)
1 teaspoon Garlic Paste (see page 22)
1 tablespoon Green Chili Paste (see page 22)
½ teaspoon ground coriander
a pinch of ground cumin
a pinch of Garam Masala (see page 24)
4 oz onions, roughly chopped
1 tablespoon tamarind paste
7 oz fresh coriander leaves
2 oz fresh mint leaves
½ teaspoon ground turmeric
2 tablespoons Cashew Nut Paste (see page 23)
3 tablespoons water
salt to taste

1 Put all the ingredients for the marinade in a blender and process to a smooth paste. Marinate the chicken in the paste for at least 6 hours.

2 Heat the vegetable oil in a deep pan, add the chicken, and deep-fry over a medium heat for about 10 minutes, until tender and cooked through. Remove from the pan, drain on paper toweling, garnish with the mint leaves, and serve immediately.

Ambotik denotes a homemade recipe for chicken or fish. The addition of tomatoes to the coconut-based gravy enhances the taste.

Ambotik

Chicken in coconut and onion gravy

1 Put the chopped onion, coriander, cumin, turmeric, paprika, chili powder, some salt, and 7 tablespoons warm water in a blender and process to a paste.

2 Heat the vegetable oil in a pan, add the sliced onion, and fry for about 5 minutes, until golden brown. Then add the paste and fry over a medium heat for about 5 minutes, until the oil separates from the mixture. Add the tomatoes and cook, stirring, for 5 minutes.

3 Add the chicken pieces and some salt and cook, stirring, for 15 minutes. Reduce the heat and add $\frac{1}{2}$ cup water and the coconut milk. Cover and cook for 20 minutes, until the chicken is tender and the oil has separated from the mixture again.

4 Stir in the coconut cream. The sauce should have a pouring consistency. Serve with plain boiled rice.

Serves 4–6

2 onions, 1 chopped and
   1 sliced
1 teaspoon ground coriander
$\frac{1}{2}$ teaspoon ground cumin
$\frac{1}{2}$ teaspoon ground turmeric
1 tablespoon paprika
$\frac{1}{2}$ teaspoon red chili powder
salt to taste
$\frac{1}{2}$ cup vegetable oil
2 tomatoes, sliced
$2\frac{1}{4}$ lb boneless chicken, cut
   into bite-sized pieces
7 tablespoons coconut milk
$\frac{7}{8}$ cup coconut cream

Balchao is a very warming dish, ideally served with *chappatis* or *poories*.

Any left over can be canned in ceramic jars, and is generally termed as pickle.

Shrimp Balchao

Spiced shrimp

Serves 4–6

5 tablespoons vegetable oil

6 cloves

2 cinnamon sticks

5 oz onions, sliced

1 tablespoon Garlic Paste (see
  page 22)

$^1/_2$ teaspoon red chili powder

$^1/_2$ teaspoon crushed black
  pepper

$^1/_2$ teaspoon ground cumin

$^1/_2$ teaspoon ground fennel
  seed

3 tablespoons malt vinegar

12 oz tomatoes, chopped

15 fresh curry leaves

4 oz jaggery

1 tablespoon brown sugar

salt to taste

$4^1/_2$ oz tomato paste

$2^1/_4$ lb medium-sized raw
  headless shrimp, shelled
  and deveined

1 Heat the oil in a deep, heavy-based pan or in a wok, add the cloves and cinnamon sticks and fry for 10 seconds, until they begin to splutter. Add the onions and cook, stirring, for 10 minutes, until they start to turn brown. Add the garlic paste and cook for 30 seconds.

2 Reduce the heat, add all the ground spices and the vinegar, and cook until the oil starts to separate from the mixture.

3 Add the chopped tomatoes, curry leaves, jaggery, brown sugar, and some salt and cook until the oil separates from the mixture again. Pour in 2 cups plus 2 tablespoons water, bring to a boil and add the tomato purée. Mix well and cook for about 15 minutes, until smooth.

4 Add the shrimp and cook for 6–8 minutes. Serve with plain boiled rice.

"मेरा जीवन ही मेरा संदेश है"

The impact of Moghlai cuisine on Hyderabad was so great that pulaos and kebabs became very popular and led to local variations, such as the famous Hyderabadi biryani.

Hyderabad

Hyderabad in Andhra Pradesh, one of the premier cities of India, was famous for its cuisine, wine, and culture. Its rulers, the Nizams, were fabulously wealthy—the sixth Nizam, for example, had a 240-foot long wardrobe for his clothes. His son was the richest man in the world, with such quantity of treasure that he stored it in trucks parked in his palace grounds. Near Hyderabad are the famous Golconda diamond mines that yielded the fabled Koh-in-Noor, whose first owner was Mir Jumla, commander of the Hyderabad fort. When the fabulous gem passed into Moghul hands, Emperor Babur estimated its value at two-and-half days food for the entire world.

The Nizam, surrounded by immensely tall Pathan bodyguards, would sometimes come to eat at the humble cafés in town. These serve authentic Hyderabadi food, dishes such as *shorva* broths, made by simmering lamb bones or poultry in huge vats with vegetables, mint, coriander, and spices; *nihari*, goat stew thickened with gram flour, cooked overnight in a sealed pot; piping hot lamb mince samosas; goat trotters (considered to be an aphrodisiac food); and a big choice of breads—*phulkas*, *kulchas*, *naan*, *tandoori parantha*, *aab-e-rawa*—many of which are cooked on charcoal fires. People on their way to work stop to eat a plate of *nihari* (lamb and lentil stew), with tandoori *roti*, for breakfast.

The eateries are close to the vegetable markets that begin trading at 4 A.M. as well as to the spice and meat markets. The penetrating smell of chilies, cumin, fenugreek, cardamom, vetiver, star anise and other spices, sold in open jute bags, pervades everything. In earlier times, the meat market sold live poultry since there were no refrigerators, but special cold rooms lined with ice were created for meat, including that of rabbit and camel.

Andhra food is hot and spicy and a recipe for mango pickle could, for example, call for equal weights of raw mango and red chilies. Tamarind is widely used. A typical Hyderabadi housewife's spicebox would include curry leaves, red chilies, mustard seeds, jaggery, peanuts, sesame seeds, cinnamon, and cumin. Meat or vegetable dishes are garnished with a *baghar* where mustard and cumin seeds, curry leaves, and red chilies are quickly fried in hot oil and poured over the simmering dish, after which it is swiftly covered to hold the flavor. The garnish helps to give it the authentic flavour of Hyderabad.

Toasted melon seeds make an attractive garnish to this dish—just wash and dry

some melon seeds and then place under a medium-hot grill until lightly roasted.

Dal Gosht

Lamb and lentil curry

1 Soak the split peas in 5 cups water for 1 hour, then drain. Put the split peas in a pan with 5 cups fresh water and boil for 20 minutes, skimming off any scum from the top. Add the turmeric and some salt and boil for another 20 minutes.

2 Heat the vegetable oil in a large pan, add the whole spices, and let them splutter for 10 seconds. Add the onions and stir-fry for 15 minutes, until golden brown.

3 Add the lamb, ginger and garlic pastes, ground spices and some salt and cook, stirring, for 25 minutes.

4 Pour in 3¹/₂ cups water, bring to a boil and cook for 20 minutes. Then add the split peas, reduce the heat to very low, and cook, covered, for 20 minutes.

5 Heat the ghee or clarified butter in a pan, add the remaining tempering ingredients, and let them splutter for 10 seconds. Pour this mixture on top of the cooked meat. Stir in the tamarind paste, fresh coriander, and green chili and simmer for 10 minutes. Sprinkle on the melon seeds, if using, and serve.

Serves 4–6

1¹/₄ lb channa dal (yellow split peas)
¹/₂ teaspoon ground turmeric
salt to taste
¹/₂ cup vegetable oil
4 cinnamon sticks
1 teaspoon green cardamom pods
1 teaspoon cloves
4 teaspoons melon seeds
5 onions, chopped
2¹/₄ lb boneless leg of lamb, cut into 1-inch cubes
2 tablespoons Ginger Paste (see page 22)
3 tablespoons Garlic Paste (see page 22)
1¹/₂ teaspoons red chili powder
2 teaspoons ground cumin
¹/₂ teaspoon ground turmeric
2 oz tamarind paste
5 tablespoons chopped fresh coriander
1¹/₂ tablespoons finely chopped green chili

For tempering:

2 oz ghee or clarified butter (see page 23)
8 dried red chilies
25 fresh curry leaves
1 tablespoon finely chopped garlic
¹/₂ teaspoon cumin seeds
¹/₄ teaspoon fenugreek seeds
1 tablespoon toasted melon seeds to garnish (optional)

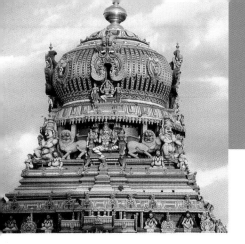

Fish curry—Hyderabadi-style—a very delectable version.

Machhli Ka Saalan

Hake in spiced coconut sauce

Serves 4–6

1 teaspoon red chili powder

¼ teaspoon ground turmeric

1 teaspoon tamarind paste

1 tablespoon ground
  coriander

1 teaspoon ground cumin

salt to taste

7 tablespoons vegetable oil

5 oz onions, sliced

1 teaspoon Ginger Paste (see
  page 22)

1 teaspoon Garlic Paste (see
  page 22)

½ teaspoon Green Chili Paste
  (see page 22)

5 oz tomatoes, chopped

1 lb 2 oz hake fillets, skinned
  and cut into 1-inch cubes
  (cod may be used)

½ cup coconut milk

slivers of fried garlic

1 tablespoon dried shre
  coconut

1 Put the chili powder, turmeric, tamarind, coriander, and cumin in a blender with 7 tablespoons water and some salt and process to a purée.

2 Heat the oil in a pan, add the onions, and fry until golden brown. Add the ginger, garlic and green chili pastes and the tomatoes and stir-fry for 2–3 minutes.

3 Add the tamarind mixture and stir-fry for another 2 minutes. Stir in 1½ cups water and bring to a boil.

4 Add the fish and cook for 10 minutes. Stir in the coconut milk and heat through but do not let it boil. Sprinkle on the slivers of fried garlic and shredded coconut and serve.

Any Indian bread goes well with this dish.

Ande Ka Khagina

Scrambled eggs with chili and coriander

1 Break the eggs into a bowl, add some salt, and whisk for 30 seconds.

2 Heat the oil in a large pan, add the onions, green chili, turmeric, chili powder, ginger, and garlic pastes and stir-fry for 1 minute.

3 Add the eggs and scramble them, then cook until any moisture has dried up. Stir in the fresh coriander and serve.

Serves 4–6

10 eggs

salt to taste

4 tablespoons vegetable oil

7 oz onions, finely chopped

1 teaspoon finely chopped green chili

a pinch of ground turmeric

¼ teaspoon red chili powder

1 teaspoon Ginger Paste (see page 22)

1 teaspoon Garlic Paste (see page 22)

3 tablespoons chopped fresh coriander

During the fasting season of Holy Ramzan, Muslims eat *Haleem* before sunrise—it is considered to be very nourishing.

Haleem

Spiced lamb with wheat

1 Mix together the lamb, yogurt, ginger and garlic pastes, and some salt and set aside for 2 hours.

2 Soak the cracked wheat in 3½ cups water for 1 hour, then drain, put in a pan and cover with fresh water. Bring to a boil and cook for about 20 minutes, until tender. Drain off excess water through a sieve.

3 Heat the ghee in a large, heavy-based pan, add the onions, and fry for about 15 minutes, until golden brown. Add the meat and cook, stirring, for 20–25 minutes, until all the natural juices dry up and the oil separates from the mixture.

4 Add the ground spices and cook for another 5 minutes, then add 5 cups water. Bring to a boil and cook, covered, for 30 minutes, stirring every 5 minutes.

5 Remove half the meat from the pan and set aside. Add the boiled wheat to the remaining meat and cook over very low heat, mashing the lamb and broken wheat constantly with a wooden spoon (or you can purée the mixture in a blender).

6 Put the cashew nuts, dried shredded coconut, and poppy seeds in a blender with 7 tablespoons water and blend to a paste. Add this to the pan with the reserved meat and continue cooking for 10–15 minutes. The mixture should have the consistency of porridge. Stir in the lemon juice and serve, garnished with the fresh coriander, mint, and fried cashew nuts.

Serves 4–6

1 lb 2 oz boneless shoulder or leg of lamb, cut into 1-inch cubes

4 tablespoons yogurt, preferably Greek yogurt, whisked

2 teaspoons Ginger Paste (see page 22)

1 tablespoon Garlic Paste (see page 22)

salt to taste

9 oz cracked wheat

4 oz ghee (see page 23)

9 oz onions, thinly sliced

1 teaspoon red chili powder

¼ teaspoon ground cloves

½ teaspoon ground cinnamon

1 teaspoon ground green cardamom

1½ oz cashew nuts

1 oz dried shredded coconut

1 teaspoon poppy seeds

1 tablespoon lemon juice

To garnish:

2 tablespoons chopped fresh coriander

1½ teaspoons chopped fresh mint

25–30 fried cashew nuts

Shiny purple eggplants are twice cooked—once in hot oil and then simmered in a sweet/sour sauce. Jaggery (below right) is sugarcane juice that is crystallized into solids.

Baghare Baingan

Eggplants in piquant sauce

1 Cut the eggplants lengthways in half but leave them attached at the stem. Heat the 3 cups oil for deep-frying over a moderate heat, add the eggplant and fry for 15 minutes. Remove and drain on paper toweling.

2 Dry-roast the onions in an oven preheated to 425°F for 30 minutes, until the skin is blackened. Peel off the top layer of each onion and set aside.

3 Heat a heavy-based frying pan over a medium heat, add all the whole spices except the mustard seeds, and dry-roast for 5 minutes. Grind to a powder.

4 Put the ground roasted spices in a blender with the roasted onions, coconut, ginger and garlic pastes, jaggery, peanuts, tamarind, turmeric, chili powder, and some salt, and blend to a smooth paste, adding up to 7 tablespoons water if necessary.

5 Heat the 5 tablespoons vegetable oil in a pan, add the mustard seeds, and let them crackle for 10 seconds. Then add the curry leaves and cook, stirring, for 5 seconds. Add the prepared paste and stir over a low heat for 10 minutes, until the oil separates from the mixture.

6 Pour in 1 cup water and bring to a boil. Add the eggplant and cook for 5 minutes. Check the seasoning and serve garnished with deep-fried shreds of leek.

Serves 4–6

1 lb 2 oz small eggplants
3 cups plus 5 tablespoons vegetable oil for deep-frying
2 onions
2 teaspoons coriander seeds
1 teaspoon cumin seeds
1/2 teaspoon sesame seeds
1/2 teaspoon poppy seeds
5–6 fenugreek seeds
4 tablespoons dried shredded coconut
2 tablespoons Ginger Paste (see page 22)
1 tablespoon Garlic Paste (see page 22)
2 oz jaggery
2 tablespoons peanuts
2 1/2 tablespoons tamarind paste
1/4 teaspoon ground turmeric
1/2 teaspoon red chili powder
salt to taste
1/2 teaspoon black mustard seeds
15–20 fresh curry leaves
1 leek, shredded and deep fried

This dish is welcome during the monsoon season, since stored green tomatoes last for months and there is no need to visit the market, which can be many miles away.

Tamatar Waale Chaawal

Tomato rice

1 Soak the rice in 5 cups water for 1 hour, then drain.

2 Finely chop half the tomatoes and cut the rest into quarters. Heat the oil in a heavy pan, add the finely chopped tomatoes, chili powder, green chilies, ginger, and some salt and stir-fry for 5 minutes.

3 Add 3 cups water and bring to a boil. Add the soaked rice and tomato quarters and bring back to a boil. Cook, stirring gently, for about 10 minutes, until the water has been absorbed.

4 Reduce the heat to very low, cover the pan with a tight-fitting lid, and cook for 15–20 minutes. Sprinkle over the lemon juice, mix into the rice, and serve.

Serves 4–6

1 lb 2 oz basmati rice
7 oz tomatoes
7 tablespoons vegetable oil
1 teaspoon red chili powder
2 green chilies, cut in half
2 tablespoons finely shredded
 fresh ginger
salt to taste
4 teaspoons lemon juice

Not only full of flavors and textures, this dish is rich in protein.

Saag Dal

Spinach with mung beans

Serves 4–6

1 lb 2 oz moong dal (yellow
  mung beans)
½ teaspoon ground turmeric
1 tablespoon Ginger Paste
  (see page 22)
2 tablespoons Garlic Paste
  (see page 22)
5 green chilies, cut in half
salt to taste
1 lb 2 oz baby spinach,
  washed
2 tablespoons lemon juice
2 tablespoons dried mango
  powder
4 oz fresh coriander, chopped

For tempering:

½ cup vegetable oil
½ teaspoon mustard seeds
½ teaspoon cumin seeds
4 dried red chilies
25–30 fresh curry leaves
1 tablespoon chopped garlic

1 Soak the mung beans in 3½ cups water for 30 minutes, then drain. Heat 5 cups water in a large pan, add the drained mung beans and bring to a boil. Boil for 10 minutes, then skim the scum from the top.

2 Add the turmeric, ginger and garlic pastes, green chilies and some salt and cook for 20 minutes. Keep cooking while you prepare the tempering.

3 Heat the vegetable oil in a pan, add the mustard seeds, cumin seeds, and dried red chilies and let them crackle for a few seconds. Then add the curry leaves and garlic and stir-fry for 10 seconds. Add the spinach and sauté for 30 seconds. Add this mixture to the mung beans and simmer for 5 minutes. Stir in the lemon juice, mango powder, and chopped fresh coriander, and serve.

Chennai

The Coromandel Coast on the east and the Malabar Coast on the western strip of South India are home to the country's most ancient race, the Dravidians, but international trade by sea was always brisk and many ancient foreigners settled there. Traders came for sesame oil, sandal, betel, muslin that was described as "webs of woven wind," salt, pepper, and other spices. The ancient Romans, Greeks, and Arabs came by sea, the Dutch, French, Portuguese, and English followed. The majority of the inhabitants are Hindus but there are big populations of Christians and Muslims and each community has its own cuisine. Syrian Christians eat beef, Kerala Muslims eat meat biryani and *harisa* (a broth of ground wheat and meat), the Hindu Nair specialities are *aviyal* (vegetables in coconut milk) and chicken cooked in coconut, the Hindu Namboodiri Brahmins, custodians of the ancient knowledge of Ayurveda, are strict vegetarians who eat rice *idli* and *dosai* for breakfast.

Ayurvedic cures involve diet, herbs, yoga, and meditation. The doctor deals with the three biological humors—*Vata*, *Pitta*, *Kapha*, i.e. air, fire, and water—which determine the forces of growth and decay in the body. Accordingly, heating and cooling foods are prescribed. The most heating foods are generally pungent, followed by sour and salty. The most cooling taste is bitter, followed by astringent and sweet. Eating sweets harmonizes the mind and promotes contentment. Salty food works as a laxative and sedative. The sour taste is both carminative and a stimulant. Bitter foods purify and detoxify. Astringent foods stop bleeding and help heal skin and mucous membrane.

Madras, which has reverted back to its old name Chennai (Beautiful City), was famous for its Udipi cuisine. The hot and sour *rassam* soup (see page 115) has always been part of the meal. In the 17th century, the English saw the Brahmin Tamil yogis drinking *mulagu-thanni* (pepper water) and adapted the concept to create mulligatawny soup. Tiffin, a light meal, was another notion adopted by the British.

South Indian food is spicy—hot food makes you sweat, thus cooling the body. Food is commonly spiced with pepper, dried red chilies, cinnamon, cloves, and star anise, and flavored with fresh curry leaves, garlic, and coconut. Cooking time for vegetables is very short and everything is eaten with rice. Banana, yam, jackfruit, and cassava grow in abundance. Meals are traditionally eaten on fresh green banana leaves, and apart from coffee, the fermented toddy and local port wine are widely drunk.

Locally known as *mulagu-tanni* (pepper water), this British Raj creation was originally

peppercorns simmered in water with coriander, salt, and turmeric—a common pick-me-up.

Mulagu-Tanni

Mulligatawny soup

1 Boil the drained soaked split peas in 7 cups water with the turmeric for about 1 hour, until they are completely soft. Transfer to a blender and purée until smooth.

2 Heat the oil in a pan, add the ginger, garlic, curry leaves, coconut, curry powder, and two-thirds of the apples and sauté for 6–8 minutes. Add the split pea purée, coconut milk, and ½ cup water and bring to a boil. Cook for 20 minutes.

3 Remove from the heat and pass through a fine sieve. Return to the pan and cook for 10 minutes. Stir in the coconut cream and lemon juice and season to taste. Add the remaining apple cubes and garnish with the curry leaves.

Serves 4–6

14 oz channa dal *(yellow split peas), soaked in cold water for 2 hours, then drained*
½ teaspoon ground turmeric
7 tablespoons vegetable oil
1½ teaspoons finely chopped fresh ginger
1 teaspoon finely chopped garlic
10–12 fresh curry leaves
4 tablespoons dried shredded coconut

1½ teaspoons Curry Powder (see page 23)
3 cooking apples, peeled, cored and cut into 1-inch cubes
½ cup coconut milk
2 tablespoons coconut cream
2 tablespoons lemon juice
curry leaves to garnish
salt to taste

This soup can be eaten as a starter,

or boiled rice can be added to it to make a main course dish.

Thakkali Rassam

Thin tomato soup

1 Heat 1 tablespoon of the oil in a pan, add the green chili and garlic pastes and sauté for 10 seconds. Then add the tomatoes and cook, stirring, for 1 minute.

2 Stir in the turmeric, chili powder, and 7 cups water. Bring to a boil, reduce the heat to very low, and simmer for 30 minutes.

3 Heat the remaining oil in a small pan, add the asafoetida and curry leaves and stir for 10 seconds. Add this mixture to the simmering tomatoes, stir in the fresh coriander, black pepper, and some salt and cook for 10 minutes.

4 Remove from the heat and let stand for 2 minutes, until all the sediment has settled down. With a ladle, remove all the liquid from the top with the coriander and curry leaves—only this liquid should be served.

Serves 4–6

2 tablespoons vegetable oil
1 green chili, seeded
½ teaspoon Garlic Paste (see page 22)
2¼ lb tomatoes, cut into quarters
a pinch of ground turmeric
¼ teaspoon red chili powder
a pinch of asafoetida
8 fresh curry leaves
1 teaspoon chopped fresh coriander
¼ teaspoon ground black pepper
salt to taste

Nilgiris is the name of a mountain range where herbs and spices grew in abundance; the local people used them all to tasty effect in this curry.

Lemon Rice

14 oz basmati rice
7 tablespoons coconut oil
4–5 dried red chilies
$^1/_2$ teaspoon mustard seeds
1 cinnamon stick
4 cloves
a pinch of asafoetida
2 tablespoons peanuts
2 tablespoons cashew nuts
$^1/_2$ teaspoon urad dal (black gram beans)
1 tablespoon chopped fresh ginger
$^1/_4$ teaspoon ground turmeric
10–12 fresh curry leaves
4 tablespoons dried shredded coconut
2 tablespoons lemon juice
salt to taste

1 Soak the rice in cold water for 30 minutes, then drain. Put it in a pan with 7 cups salted water and boil for 8–10 minutes. It should be slightly undercooked. Drain well and set aside.

2 Heat the oil in a pan, add the whole spices, asafoetida, peanuts, cashew nuts and black gram beans and let them splutter for 15 seconds. Add the ginger, turmeric, and curry leaves and stir-fry for 10 seconds. Stir in the boiled rice, dried shredded coconut and some salt and toss until the rice is thoroughly heated. Do this gently or the grains of rice will break. Sprinkle over the lemon juice, mix well and serve.

Nilgiri Korma

Nilgiri lamb korma

1 Put the ginger, garlic, green chilies, coriander, mint and 1 cup water in a blender and process to a smooth paste, then set aside. Put the fried cashew nuts in the blender with $^1/_2$ cup water and purée, then set aside.

2 Heat the oil in a pan, add the whole spices, and let them crackle for 10 seconds. Then add the onions and fry until golden brown.

3 Add the meat, ground coriander, chili powder, dried shredded coconut, and some salt and cook, stirring, for about 20 minutes, until all the juices from the meat dry up.

4 Reduce the heat, add the green paste and cashew nut paste and cook, stirring, for about 20 minutes, until the oil separates from the mixture.

5 Pour in the coconut milk and $3^1/_2$ cups water. Bring to a boil and cook for 25 minutes, then stir in the garam masala. Garnish with the ginger strips and serve.

Serves 4–6

1 tablespoon chopped fresh ginger
2 tablespoons chopped garlic
2 green chilies, seeded and chopped
7 oz fresh coriander
4 oz fresh mint
4 oz cashew nuts, fried
$^1/_2$ cup vegetable oil
1 cinnamon stick
6 cloves
1 star anise
7 oz onions, sliced
$2^1/_4$ lb boneless leg of lamb, cut into bite-sized pieces
1 teaspoon ground coriander
$^1/_2$ teaspoon red chili powder
5 oz dried shredded coconut
$^1/_2$ cup coconut milk
salt to taste
$^1/_4$ teaspoon Garam Masala (see page 24)
large knob of fresh ginger, cut into julienne strips

English names for ingredients are fairly common in South India—a legacy of the British Raj—hence this dish is called the same in Tamil.

Coconut Lamb Fry

Lamb with coconut and coriander

1 Heat the coconut oil in a pan, add the mustard seeds and fenugreek seeds, and let them splutter for 15 seconds. Add the onions and cook, stirring, for 10 minutes or until golden brown.

2 Add the curry leaves, turmeric, ginger, garlic, green chili, ground coriander, lamb, and some salt. Cook, stirring, over a low heat for 20–25 minutes, until all the juices from the meat have dried up.

3 Add the tomatoes and coconut milk and cook until the oil separates from the mixture. Stir in the dried shredded coconut and fresh coriander. Serve with bread.

Serves 4–6

½ cup coconut oil
½ teaspoon mustard seeds
6–8 fenugreek seeds
5 oz onions, chopped
10–12 fresh curry leaves
½ teaspoon ground turmeric
2 teaspoons finely chopped
  fresh ginger
1 teaspoon finely chopped
  garlic
½ teaspoon finely chopped
  green chili
1 teaspoon ground coriander
2¼ lb boneless leg of lamb,
  cut into bite-sized pieces
salt to taste
4 oz fresh tomatoes, puréed
½ cup coconut milk
5 oz dried shredded coconut
2 tablespoons chopped fresh
  coriander

Madras has an abundance of coconut trees, and fresh coconut flesh, diced or shredded, is used rather than dried coconut.

Ginger Chicken

1 Heat the sesame oil and vegetable oil in a pan, add the onion seeds, and let them crackle for 10 seconds. Add the chilies and cook for 10 seconds, then add the onions and stir-fry for 5 minutes, until golden brown.

2 Add the ginger, curry leaves, green chili, chicken, turmeric and some salt and cook, stirring, for 10 minutes.

3 Add the tomatoes and cook, stirring, for another 10 minutes. Add the honey and chopped fresh coriander, mix well, and serve.

Serves 4–6

2 fl oz sesame oil
7 tablespoons vegetable oil
a pinch of onion seeds (nigella seeds)
6 rassampatti chilies or other hot dried red chilies
5 oz onions, chopped
1 tablespoon chopped fresh ginger
10 fresh curry leaves
1 teaspoon seeded and finely chopped green chilli

2¼ lb boneless chicken, cut into bite-sized pieces
a pinch of ground turmeric
salt to taste
4 oz tomatoes, chopped
¼ teaspoon honey
2 teaspoons chopped fresh coriander

Sambhar

Sour lentil curry with vegetables

1 Soak the lentils in 3½ cups water for 30 minutes, then drain and put them in a pan with 2 cups fresh water. Add the turmeric, bring to a boil, and cook for 30 minutes, until tender.

2 Heat the oil in a separate pan, add the mustard seeds and let them crackle for 10 seconds. Add the curry leaves and asafoetida and stir for 10 seconds.

3 Add the vegetables, sambhar powder, and some salt and sauté for 2 minutes. Add the cooked lentils, tamarind paste, jaggery, and grated coconut, bring to a boil and cook for 10 minutes.

Serves 4–6

7 oz toor dal (large yellow lentils)
½ teaspoon ground turmeric
5 tablespoons vegetable oil
½ teaspoon mustard seeds
10 fresh curry leaves
2 pinches of asafoetida
1 green drumstick, cut into 1-inch pieces
1 onion, cut into 1-inch dice
2 tomatoes, cut into quarters
2 small eggplant, cut into quarters
2 tablespoons diced pumpkin, preferably white, cut in 1-inch cubes

4 okra, cut in half lengthwise
2 tablespoons Sambhar Powder (see page 24)
salt to taste
2½ teaspoons tamarind paste
½-inch piece of jaggery
2 tablespoons grated fresh coconut

Outdoor cooking, especially in hill districts, is popular in summer. The British termed them as "camp tiffins."

Pepper is used extensively in southern India, where temperatures are high.

It helps to lower body temperature by making you drink more water.

Chicken Pepper Fry

1 Heat the coconut oil in a pan, add the cumin seeds and mustard seeds, and let them splutter for 5 seconds. Add the onions and stir-fry for 10 minutes, until they start to turn brown.

2 Add the ginger and garlic pastes, the green chili, and the curry leaves and stir-fry for 2 minutes. Add the chicken, ground coriander, turmeric, cumin, and some salt and stir-fry for 5 minutes.

3 When the juices from the chicken have dried up, add the tomatoes and stir-fry for 5 minutes. Cook over medium low heat for about 10 minutes, until the oil separates from the mixture and the liquid dries up. Stir in the lemon juice and crushed black pepper, then serve with bread.

Serves 4–6

7 tablespoons coconut oil
½ teaspoon cumin seeds
½ teaspoon mustard seeds
7 oz onions, chopped
2 teaspoons Ginger Paste (see page 22)
1 teaspoon Garlic Paste (see page 22)
1 teaspoon finely chopped green chili
10–12 fresh curry leaves
2¼ lb boneless chicken, cut into bite-sized pieces
1 teaspoon ground coriander
½ teaspoon ground turmeric
½ teaspoon ground cumin
salt to taste
5 oz tomatoes, chopped
1 tablespoon lemon juice
½ teaspoon crushed black pepper

The Malabar sea coast boasts the longest stretch of beach
in the world—spanning nearly six states.

The coconut palms of India's coastline provide the coconut oil and milk so often used in Indian cooking. Here, fresh shrimp are combined with the flavor of coconut to make a very quick and tasty meal.

Malabar Shrimp Curry

1 Heat the coconut oil over low heat, add the whole spices and let them splutter for 15 seconds. Add the onion and sauté for 5 minutes, until it becomes limp and starts to change color.

2 Stir in the ginger, garlic, green chili, and curry leaves and sauté for 2 minutes. Add the puréed tomato, ground spices and some salt and sauté until the oil separates from the mixture.

3 Push a small bamboo stick through the length of each shrimp to keep them straight while they are cooking. Add the shrimp to the mixture and stir-fry over a high heat for 2 minutes. Then add the coconut milk and bring to a boil.

4 Cook for 1 minute, remove from the heat, and stir in the coconut cream. Serve with rice.

Serves 4–6

½ cup coconut oil
6 green cardamom pods
5 cloves
3 cinnamon sticks
5 tablespoons finely chopped onion
1 teaspoon finely chopped fresh ginger
1 teaspoon finely chopped garlic
½ teaspoon finely chopped green chili
8–10 fresh curry leaves
5 tablespoons puréed fresh tomato
½ teaspoon ground coriander
¼ teaspoon red chili powder
¼ teaspoon ground turmeric
salt to taste
2¼ lb raw shrimp, shelled but leaving tails on, cleaned and deveined
8 tablespoons coconut milk
3 tablespoons coconut cream

Sesame Rice

9 oz basmati rice
1 tablespoon sesame oil
2 tablespoons vegetable oil
¼ teaspoon black sesame seeds
1 tablespoons crushed peanuts
salt to taste

1 Soak the rice in 3½ cups cold water for 30 minutes, then drain well and set aside.

2 Heat the sesame oil and vegetable oil in a pan, add the sesame seeds and crushed peanuts and let them crackle for 5 seconds. Add the drained rice and stir for 1 minute.

3 Add 1¼ cups water, bring to a boil and simmer until the rice has absorbed most of the water. Cover with foil, place in an oven preheated to 400°F and cook for 25 minutes.

Poriyal literally means "stir-fry" in Tamil. All leafy vegetables can be prepared in this manner. Madras Potatoes are eaten with rice pancakes, *dosa*, for breakfast in Madras.

Cabbage Poriyal

1 Heat the coconut oil over low heat, add the black gram beans, and cumin and mustard seeds, and let them crackle for 15 seconds. Add the onions and stir-fry for 5 minutes, until they are limp but not colored.

2 Add the ginger, garlic, curry leaves, and green chili and sauté for 1 minute. Increase the heat and add the cabbage and some salt. Stir-fry until the cabbage is hot but still crisp. Be careful that it doesn't start to give off any liquid; if it does, cook until it has evaporated.

3 Add the dried shredded coconut, chopped fresh coriander, and lemon juice and mix well.

Serves 4–6

5 tablespoons coconut oil
$^1/_2$ teaspoon urad dal *(black gram beans)*
$^1/_2$ teaspoon cumin seeds
$^1/_2$ teaspoon black mustard seeds
5 oz onions, chopped
2 teaspoons finely chopped fresh ginger
1 teaspoon finely chopped garlic
10–12 fresh curry leaves
$^1/_2$ teaspoon finely chopped green chili
2$^1/_4$ lb white cabbage, shredded
salt to taste
8 tablespoons dried shredded coconut
4 tablespoons chopped fresh coriander
1 tablespoon lemon juice

Madras Potatoes

1 Boil the potatoes in salted water with the turmeric until they are just cooked but still a little crunchy. Drain well.

2 Heat the vegetable oil in a large pan, add the potatoes, and deep-fry until crisp. Remove the potatoes from the pan and drain on paper toweling.

3 Heat the coconut oil in a large pan, add the mustard seeds and let them crackle for 5 seconds. Then add the curry leaves and fry for 5 seconds.

4 Stir in the chili powder and cumin and fry for 2 seconds. Add the potatoes and toss them in the spices, then stir in the chopped fresh coriander and lemon juice.

Serves 4–6

1 lb 2 oz small new potatoes, peeled and cut in half
a pinch of ground turmeric
3$^1/_2$ cups vegetable oil
2 tablespoons coconut oil
$^1/_4$ teaspoon black mustard seeds
6 fresh curry leaves
2 pinches of red chili powder
$^1/_2$ teaspoon ground cumin
2 tablespoons chopped fresh coriander
$^1/_2$ teaspoon lemon juice

Vegetables form a major part of South Indian meals—numerous
varieties are sold each day from woven palmleaf baskets,
precariously perched on the padded heads of the hawkers.

In India, no marriage ceremony is complete without the bride feeding the groom a sweetmeat – and vice versa.

Breads, Chutneys, and Sweets

Good to eat at any time, these accompaniments are extremely popular in India and, as with other dishes, they vary from region to region.

In India breads are planned and baked with consideration for the occasion and mood. *Pooris* are usually eaten for lunch, *chappatis* or *rotis* accompany a hearty meal, filled *naans* are eaten as snacks, and sweet breads are for celebrations. Almost all restaurants in Northern India have a tandoor oven, and bake their breads to order. Since most Indian bread is unleavened and rolled out flat, it cooks quickly, and in most Indian homes the *roti* is cooked when the meal is being served so that it can be eaten hot.

Chutneys play a major part in any meal in India. They can either be made fresh—with any available ingredients such as roasted lentils, roasted sesame seeds, fresh coriander, coconut, or even onions—or, if cooked, they can be canned. Canned chutneys are long lasting and are made from ingredients such as mangoes, garlic, tomatoes, eggplants, limes, lemons, or mixed vegetables.

The spices used in every chutney are particular to it and are chosen to enhance the flavor of that particular fruit or vegetable; for example, ajwain spice is used in oily chutney to help people digest the oil; lentil-based chutneys include asafoetida to prevent gastric problems; and winter chutneys call for green chilies or black pepper, which help to give some immunity against winter colds.

Sweets are the food of the gods. Benares, city of gods, has a huge variety, and some, such as *malai poori* (thick cream served like a pancake on a leaf plate), are particular to that city. In Punjab sweets tend to be rich, such as *halwa*; Bengalis use *chenna* (cottage cheese) and date palm molasses; and Goan housewives use a great deal of coconut in their sweets. Parsee sweets such as *malai na khaja* (a type of baklava) reflect their Persian origins, while *kulfi* (Indian ice cream) was popular with Moghuls but today is widely eaten all over India.

Breads

Bread is an essential part of every meal for nearly half the population of India—a staggering 530 million people. The rest are rice eaters.

The bread eaten in India today is almost the same as the bread baked for ancient rulers, with the same basic ingredients being used—flour, water and a leavening agent. Although India has western-style bread, called *double-roti*, the word "bread" is not really appropriate for the dozens of varieties of *rotis* eaten all over the country.

The oldest Indian *roti* is the flat tandoori *roti*, which for over five thousand years has been baked in the tandoor oven. Tandoori *roti*, tandoori *parantha*, and *naan* have always been popular, but *rotis* are also fried and roasted, such as the immensely popular *pooris* and *paranthas*. *Poori-aloo* (*poori* with potato curry) is a meal in itself, as is stuffed *parantha* with yogurt and pickles. *Pooris* can be stuffed with lentils and spices, and are deep-fried in a *kadai* (deep wok); *paranthas* can be stuffed with almost anything and are shallow-fried on a *taiwa* (iron griddle).

Rotis can also be sweet. Peshawari *naan*, for example, is a sweet *naan* made with cardamom and nuts. Sweet *paranthas*, layered with sugar that melts during cooking, are popular with children.

Naan

Leavened flat bread

1 Put the flour, salt, and baking soda in a bowl and mix well. Whisk together the yogurt, milk, sugar, and egg and mix with the flour to form a soft dough. Turn out onto a lightly floured surface and knead for 3 minutes.

2 Add the oil and knead for another 2 minutes, then cover with plastic wrap and chill for 30 minutes.

3 Divide the dough into 15 balls and dot each one with the onion seeds. Flatten the dough balls with your hand and stretch into "tear-drop" shapes (or roll out into ovals with a rolling pin), about ¼ inch thick.

4 Cook in an oven preheated to 475°F for 5–7 minutes, or in a hot tandoor oven for 2 minutes, until the *naan* are soft, fluffy, and patched with brown.

Serves 4–6

9 oz all-purpose flour
a pinch of salt
¼ teaspoon baking soda
1 tablespoon yogurt,
   preferably Greek yogurt
½ cup milk
1 tablespoon granulated sugar
½ beaten egg
1½ tablespoons vegetable oil
1½ teaspoons onion seeds
   (nigella seeds)

If you have the time, bread always tastes better if the dough is allowed to rest for at least an hour after kneading, and for *naan* about six hours is preferable.

Roti

Unleavened
whole wheat flat bread

Serves 4–6
9 oz whole wheat flour
a pinch of salt

1 Put the flour into a bowl and mix in the salt. Pour in ½ cup water and mix until soft. Turn out onto a lightly floured surface and knead for 5 minutes, until smooth and elastic. Cover with plastic wrap and chill for 30 minutes.

2 Divide the dough into 12 balls. Flatten each one with the palm of your hand and then roll out into a 6-inch circle.

3 Cook on preheated baking sheets in an oven preheated to 2475°F for 3–4 minutes, or on a hot griddle for 1 minute per side (or in a hot tandoor oven for 45 seconds). When they are done, the *roti* should be slightly puffy and speckled with brown.

Chappati

Unleavened whole wheat puffed bread

Serves 4–6
9 oz whole wheat flour
a pinch of salt

1 Put the flour into a bowl and mix in the salt. Pour in ½ cup water and mix until soft. Turn out on to a lightly floured work surface and knead for 5 minutes. Cover with plastic wrap and chill for 30 minutes.

2 Divide the dough into 20 balls. Flatten each one with the palm of your hand, then roll out into a 6-inch circle.

3 Cook each *chappati* on a flat griddle over high heat for 1 minute, flip over, and cook the other side for 2 minutes. Turn again and cook until the *chappati* puffs up.

Left A selection of Indian breads

The best breads are always freshly baked. In India a family member will bake and serve the bread while the others are eating.

Lightly fried breads are usually eaten for breakfast,

or to accompany seafood.

Poori

Deep-fried puffy bread

1 Mix the flour, salt, and melted ghee together and add 7 tablespoons water to make a fairly stiff dough. Cover with plastic wrap and chill for 30 minutes.

2 Divide the dough into 25 balls. Flatten each one with the palm of your hand and then roll out into a 4-inch circle.

3 Heat the oil for deep-frying over a moderate heat and fry the *poori* on both sides until they puff up. Remove from the pan and drain in a colander.

Serves 4–6

9 oz whole wheat flour
a pinch of salt
1 tablespoon ghee, melted (see page 23)
3¹/₂ cups vegetable oil for deep-frying

Parantha

Whole wheat flaky bread

1 Put the flour in a bowl and mix in the salt. Pour in 7 tablespoons water and stir together into a fairly stiff dough. Turn out on to a lightly floured surface and knead for 3 minutes, then wrap in plastic wrap and chill for 30 minutes.

2 Divide the dough into 12 balls. Flatten each one with the palm of your hand and then roll out into a 6-inch circle. Brush with ghee and sprinkle a little flour over the top. Fold the dough into a semicircle and then fold it again to form a triangle. Cover with plastic wrap and chill for 10 minutes.

3 Roll out each triangle into a bigger triangle about ¹/₄-inch thick. Place on preheated baking sheets and cook in an oven preheated to 475°F for 8–10 minutes, or on a hot griddle for 2 minutes per side (or in a hot tandoor oven for 1¹/₂–2 minutes), until the *paranthas* are golden brown.

Serves 4–6

9 oz whole wheat flour, plus extra for sprinkling
a pinch of salt
2 oz ghee (see page 23)

Chutneys

Indians enjoy eating accompaniments such as pickles, chutneys, *papad*, fresh green chilies, and *kachumbar* (chopped raw onion and tomato) with their meals or snacks. Family recipes for pickles and chutneys are often kept secret and passed down through the generations as heirlooms, forming part of the family history.

    Hinduism says a meal should have the six *rasas* (tastes): sweet, salty, bitter, pungent, sour, and spicy. Chutneys can be all these things and, thus, they can help to balance the meal. They also stimulate the appetite and help digestion.

Gajar ki Chutney

Carrot chutney

Serves 4–6

1 lb 2 oz carrots, grated
3 oz granulated sugar
$^7/_8$ cup white vinegar
2 green cardamom pods, lightly crushed

a pinch of ground fennel seeds
salt to taste
$^1/_4$ teaspoon onion seeds (nigella seeds)

1 Put all the ingredients except the onion seeds in a pan and mix well. Bring to a boil and cook for 1 minute.

2 Stir in the onion seeds and cook for 1 minute, then remove from the heat, and cool.

Pudiney ki Chutney

Mint chutney

Serves 4–6

9 oz fresh coriander leaves
$4^1/_2$ oz mint leaves
2 oz yogurt, preferably Greek yogurt
1 tablespoon dried mango powder

1 green chili, seeded and chopped
$^1/_2$ teaspoon finely chopped fresh ginger
1 tablespoon granulated sugar
salt to taste

1 Put all the ingredients in a blender or food processor and mix to a smooth paste.

Nariyal ki Chutney

Coconut chutney

Serves 4–6

1 lb 2 oz coconut, freshly grated
2 green chilies, chopped
7 oz roasted channa dal

1 tablespoon coconut oil
$^1/_2$ teaspoon mustard seeds
10–15 fresh curry leaves
salt to taste

1 Put the coconut, green chilies, *channa dal*, salt and $^7/_8$ cup water in a blender or food processor and mix to a smooth paste. Transfer to a bowl.

2 Heat the coconut oil in a small pan and add the mustard seeds. Cook for 10 seconds, until they start to splutter, then add the curry leaves and cook for 5 seconds longer. Pour this mixture onto the chutney and stir it in. Serve chilled.

One of the most popular chutneys, mango chutney can be canned and stored.

Mint chutney, however, should be eaten fresh since it is not cooked.

A a m   k i   C h u t n e y

Mango chutney

Serves 4–6

1 lb 2 oz diced mango

4 oz granulated sugar

1 teaspoon salt

$\frac{1}{2}$ teaspoon cumin seeds, dry roasted in a frying pan and then ground

2 teaspoons lemon juice

$\frac{1}{2}$ teaspoon finely chopped fresh ginger

$\frac{1}{2}$ teaspoon dried red chili flakes

a pinch of onion seeds (nigella seeds)

2 green cardamom pods

2 cloves

1 Put all the ingredients in a pan. Add $\frac{7}{8}$ cup water and bring to a boil.

2 Reduce the heat and cook for 5 minutes over very low heat. Remove and set aside to cool.

T a m a t a r   k i   C h u t n e y

Tomato chutney

Serves 4–6

1 tablespoon vegetable oil

$\frac{1}{4}$ teaspoon black mustard seeds

10–12 fresh curry leaves

$\frac{1}{4}$ teaspoon Ginger Paste (see page 22)

$\frac{1}{4}$ teaspoon Garlic Paste (see page 22)

6 tablespoons thick tomato paste

1 tablespoon vinegar

1 teaspoon granulated sugar

salt to taste

1 Heat the oil in a pan, add the mustard seeds, and sizzle for 10 seconds. Add the curry leaves and stir for 5 seconds. Add the ginger and garlic and stir for 15 seconds. Then add all the remaining ingredients and bring to a boil. Cook for 2 minutes, remove from the heat, and cool.

Sweets

Indian sweets have a symbolic significance that goes beyond the physical act of eating them. On hearing happy news, the first reaction is, "*Muh meetha karo!*"—eat something sweet.

Most Indian *mithai* (sweets) are milk-based, using *chenna* (a type of cottage cheese) or *khoya* (reduced milk). Cereals such as wheat flour, rice, lentils, and semolina are also used but the most popular is *besan* (gram flour). Coconut, mango, carrots, gourd, figs, oranges, saffron, *keora* (vetiver), rose water, almonds, pistachios—anything and everything can be used for taste and flavor. Sugar toys, made by pouring sugar syrup into molds, are made for the Diwali festival in autumn and are very popular with children. They are shaped like birds and trees, or can even be in the form of Mahatma Gandhi, the father of the nation.

Then there are the nursery puddings and Club desserts, such as soufflé, bread-and-butter pudding, and caramel custard, which are among the few culinary legacies left behind by the British Raj. At first it was a struggle to produce puddings in wood-fired ovens, but gradually, given the abundance of ingredients, successful Anglo-Indian variations appeared. Even today, old *khansamers* in army messes continue to produce light soufflés that the *burra memsahib* would have approved of.

Phirni

Almond rice pudding

1 Put the rice in a bowl, pour over ⅞ cup water and let soak for 30 minutes. Pour into a blender and process to a paste.

2 Put the milk in a pan and bring to a boil. Add the cardamom, reduce the heat to low and simmer for 5 minutes. Add the rice paste and simmer for 15 minutes, stirring constantly.

3 Stir in the sugar, almonds, and raisins and simmer for 10 minutes. Pour into a bowl and leave to cool, then chill before serving.

Serves 4–6

3 oz basmati rice
3½ cups whole milk
2 green cardamom pods, crushed
5 oz granulated sugar
2 tablespoons thinly sliced almonds
1 tablespoon raisins

Gujarat is well known for its *Shrikhand*. All festivities are celebrated with great pomp,

and feasts are served—*Shrikhand* is one of the essential sweet elements.

Shrikhand

Yogurt with nuts

Serves 4–6

7 cups skimmed milk

½ teaspoon set yogurt

½ cup granulated sugar,
  powdered in a blender

a pinch of ground green
  cardamom

2 teaspoons crushed cashew
  nuts

1 teaspoon crushed pistachio
  nuts

1 teaspoon crushed charoli
  nuts

3 tablespoons light cream

1 Put the milk in a pan and bring to a boil, remove from heat and cool to body temperature (98°F/37°C). Stir in the yogurt, cover with a lid and leave in a warm place overnight to set—you could wrap the bowl in a blanket and leave it in a warm room. Alternatively, pour it into a yogurt-making machine and follow the manufacturer's instructions. Once it has set into yogurt, transfer to the refrigerator and let it chill for 6 hours or until firm.

2 Put the yogurt into a piece of cheesecloth, taking care not to break the set curds. Tie up the ends and hang it up in a cool place for 8–10 hours or overnight to drain off all the whey.

3 Stir in the sugar and ground cardamom and then beat the yogurt with a whisk until it becomes soft and fluffy, like cream cheese. Mix in the nuts and cream and then chill. Just before serving, beat it again.

Rice puddings are universally eaten in South India and always on auspicious occasions.

In tropical heat, a bowl of chilled *Phirni* is heavenly.

It is a popular dessert for festivals and weddings.

Aam Phirni

Rice pudding with mangoes and nuts

1 Put the rice in a bowl, pour over 7 tablespoons water and let soak for 30 minutes. Pour into a blender and process to a paste.

2 Put the milk in a pan and bring to a boil. Add the cardamom, reduce the heat to low and simmer for 5 minutes. Add the rice paste and simmer for 15 minutes, stirring constantly.

3 Stir in the sugar, almonds, and raisins and simmer for 10 minutes. Pour into a bowl and let cool, then chill. Stir in the mango purée, diced mango, and cashew nuts, and garnish with the silver leaf and pistachios, if using.

Serves 4–6

3 oz basmati rice
3¹/₂ cups whole milk
2 green cardamom pods, crushed
5 oz granulated sugar
2 tablespoons flaked almonds
1 tablespoon raisins
4 oz mango purée

5 oz mango, cut into ¹/₂-inch cubes
2 tablespoons crushed cashew nuts
silver leaf and slivers of shelled pistachios, to garnish (optional)

Kheer

Crushed rice pudding with nuts and raisins

1 Put the rice in a bowl and pour over 1 cup water. Let to soak for 1 hour, then drain.

2 Put the milk in a pan, bring to a boil, then reduce the heat to low and simmer for 5 minutes. Add the drained rice and return to a boil. Cook for 15 minutes, stirring constantly.

3 Add all the remaining ingredients and cook for another 10 minutes. Serve hot or cold.

Serves 4–6

4¹/₂ oz basmati rice
5¹/₂ cups skim milk
5 oz granulated sugar
2 tablespoons thinly sliced almonds
2 tablespoons raisins
3 green cardamom pods, crushed

Left Aam Phirni

Shahi Tukra is bread pudding Hyderabadi-style.
It is usually served decorated with pure beaten silver
wrapped on sweetmeats.

Use cold toast instead of fried bread for the *Shahi Tukra*, if preferred.

Or bread rusks can also be used.

Shahi Tukra

Royal pudding

1 Cut the crusts off the bread and cut each slice into 4 triangles. Heat the oil for deep-frying and fry the bread triangles over a low heat until golden. Drain on kitchen paper and set aside.

2 Put the milk in a pan, bring to a boil, and add the sugar and cardamom. Reduce the heat to low and cook for 15 minutes, then remove from the heat. Soak the fried bread triangles in the milk for 10 seconds, remove with a slotted spoon and arrange in a serving dish.

3 Boil the milk, stirring occasionally, until it has reduced in volume by three-quarters. Remove from the heat and cool. Stir in the rosewater and pour the reduced milk over the fried bread triangles. Sprinkle over the nuts, garnish with the rose petals if using, and serve cold.

Serves 4–6

4 *slices of white bread, cut 1-inch thick*

3 1/2 *cups vegetable oil for deep-frying*

7 *cups skim milk*

2 *oz granulated sugar*

2 *green cardamom pods, crushed*

1/4 *teaspoon rosewater*

1 *teaspoon crushed pistachio nuts*

1 *teaspoon crushed almonds*

fresh rose petals, to garnish (optional)

Seviyan

Sweet vermicelli

1 Put the milk in a pan, bring to a boil and add the cardamom. Reduce the heat to low and cook for 10 minutes.

2 Stir in the vermicelli and sugar and return to a boil. Cook for 5 minutes. Serve hot or cold.

Serves 4–6

3 1/2 *cups milk*

2 *green cardamom pods, crushed*

4 *oz angel's hair vermicelli (seviyan)*

5 *oz granulated sugar*

Left Shahi Tukra

Glossary

Aniseed distinctive flavoring agent, licorice-like taste.

Asafoetida dried resin available in lump form or powdered; used as a digestive spice, it has a strong aroma.

Basmati rice a long-grained, fine-textured rice, it has a nutty flavor.

Black gram beans (urad dal) protein-rich bean, with white seed.

Black salt naturally occuring salt in the form of rocks. Its powdered form is pink. It is stronger than common salt and has a distinct flavor.

Carom seeds (ajwain) small, yellowish seeds that have a sharp and piquant taste, with a fragrance similar to thyme when crushed.

Cardamom (pods and ground, green and black) a flavoring spice, it is delicately perfumed.

Cassia buds available dried or fresh, they have a flavor similar to cloves, nutmeg and cinnamon.

Channa dal yellow split peas. Roasted channa dal is channa dal which has been soaked and dry roasted. It can be eaten as a snack or used in powdered/paste form.

Charoli nuts small round nuts with a subtle flavor.

Chili powder ground, dried red chilies; heat varies according to what type of chili has been used.

Cinnamon (sticks or ground) the inner bark of a tree, it imparts a fragrant, slightly sweet flavor. The sticks are inedible and should be removed from the dish before eating.

Cloves (whole and ground) dried plant buds, with a strong flavor.

Coconuts/coconut oil the fruit of the coconut palm; the creamy coconut meat is pressed to make coconut oil. Coconut is high in saturated fat.

Coriander (leaves and seeds, whole and ground) the fresh leaves have a distinctive smell and flavor, and resemble flat-leafed parsley. The seeds have a milder and sweeter flavor.

Curry leaves small, bright green, shiny leaves that impart a strong curry flavor. Dried curry leaves are also available, but fresh are preferable.

Fennel seeds (whole and ground) delicately flavored, slightly aniseedy spice.

Fenugreek leaves and seeds (whole and ground) the leaves have a flavor similar to mint. The seeds have a very strong flavor. Both are bitter in taste and should be used with care.

Garam masala spice mix (*see page* 24).

Ghee a variant of clarified butter (*see page* 23).

Ginger (fresh and dried ground) fresh ginger is a knobbly root which, when peeled, yields a fibrous pale yellow flesh. It has a spicy flavor; always try to use fresh ginger where a recipe specifies it, rather than dried ground. Dried ground ginger has an earthier quality to its flavor.

Gourds (wax, bitter, bottle, snake) long cylindrical vegetables, related to the squash family, the varieties vary in size and weight. Most have a central seed core and firm skin.

Gram flour chickpea flour.

Green chilies hot peppers, not to be confused with green peppers. The inner seeds and membrane of the chili contain the most heat; all the flesh contains a volatile oil which results in burning of eyes or skin if care is not taken. Use with caution.

Green drumstick long, round bean-like vegetable, that tastes similar to squash. Cut into lengths, cook and then peel.

Jaggery also known as palm sugar, sugarcane juice that is crystallized into solids. It has a strong flavor. Brown sugar can also be used.

Lentils (red, green, and yellow) rich in protein, vitamins and minerals, these pulses are extremely versatile.

Mango, dried powder (amchoor) ground dried, unripe mango, used to give a raw mango/sour flavor. Lemon or lime juice can be used as a substitute.

Mustard oil a pungently flavored oil, extracted from mustard seeds; invaluable in pickling; when heated it has a sweetish flavor.

Mustard seeds brown or black seeds of mustard plant; have a pungent, strong flavor.

Paneer firm cottage cheese, rich in protein. Available cubed.

Pomegranate seeds available whole or powdered, they have a sweet/sour flavor.

Rosewater diluted rose essence – fragrant liquid extracted from rose petals; used in puddings and drinks.

Rice flour a thickening agent made from white rice. Different from sweet rice flour.

Saffron dried stigmas of flowers of saffron plant; strong flavoring and coloring agent. Available in strands or ground – strands are better.

Stoneflower (paththar ke phool) a kind of lichen that grows on rocks and stones. When whole, it is used with other whole spices, tied in a cheesecloth and immersed in the liquid for a slow infusion. When powdered, it should be used at the end of cooking.

Tamarind (pulp) a souring and coloring agent. Also available in blocks, dark brown in color, resembling dates.

Tempering addition to a dish of whole or ground spices fried in very hot oil.

Turmeric (ground) the ground root of a rhizome, this yellow spice is used as a flavoring and coloring agent; strongly flavored, peppery taste.

Vetiver a mild and highly aromatic root. Also available bottled, from Asian stores, as an extract, when it is used in desserts.

Yogurt fermented milk, indispensable in Indian cooking; it acts as a marinade, aids digestion and is invaluable in sauces.

Index

Copyright

First published in the United States in 2002 by Periplus Editions (HK) Ltd., with editorial offices at 153 Milk Street, Boston, Massachusetts 02109.

FOOD STYLING, ART DIRECTION, AND DESIGN CONCEPT:
New Crane Communications Ltd.
Food photographs: Philip Webb
Styling: Helen Trent

FOR HARPERCOLLINS*PUBLISHERS*:
COMMISSIONING EDITOR: Barbara Dixon
DESIGN MANAGER: Mabel Chan
DESIGNER: Mark Stevens
INDEXER: Susan Bosanko

ISBN 0-79465-017-1
Library of Congress Control Number: 2002102161

Distributed By

North America
Tuttle Publishing
Distribution Center
Airport Industrial Park
364 Innovation Drive
North Clarendon, VT 05759-9436
Tel: (802) 773-8930
Tel: (800) 526-2778
Fax: (802) 773-6993

Japan
Tuttle Publishing
RK Building, 2nd Floor
2-13-10 Shimo-Meguro
Meguro-ku
Tokyo 153 0064
Tel: (03) 5437-0171
Tel: (03) 5437-0755

Asia Pacific
Berkeley Books Pte. Ltd.
130 Joo Seng Road
#06-01/03
Olivine Building
Singapore 368357
Tel: (65) 280-1330
Fax: (65) 280-6290

First Edition
05 04 03 02   9 8 7 6 5 4 3 2 1
Printed in the United Kingdom